THE AMERICAN CAUSE

THE AMERICAN CAUSE

Russell Kirk

*Edited with a New Introduction
by Gleaves Whitney*

ISI BOOKS
Wilmington, Delaware
2002

Cataloging-in-Publication Data

Kirk, Russell.
     The American cause / Russell Kirk ;
    edited , with a new introduction by Gleaves
    Whitney. —3rd ed. —Wilmington, DE : ISI Books, 2002.

       p. ; cm.

    ISBN 1-882926-93-5 (pbk.)
      1. United States—Civilization. 2.
    United States—History—Philosophy. 3. Communism. I.
Title.

    E169.1 .K57 2002   2002107933
    973–dc21   0209

Published in the United States by:
        ISI Books
        P.O. Box 4431
        Wilmington, DE 19807-0431

Acknowledgments

The idea of editing this book grew out of two conversations. The first was with Russell Kirk's wife Annette on August 1, 1998. It was a spectacularly beautiful Michigan day, not at all hot or humid, and we were enjoying lunch on the terrace at St. Ives in the Canadian Lakes (near the Kirk ancestral home, Piety Hill). I was briefing Annette and her brother Regis Courtemanche on the lectures I was developing around Russell Kirk's masterful survey of Western civilization, *The Roots of American Order*. Annette ventured that at some point I might be interested in editing a new edition of Kirk's earlier book called *The American Cause*, since it was in some ways the forerunner of *Roots*. I agreed that the connection was important, but was not sure when I could devote the time to tackle it.

Then came September 11th. Suddenly the time—in the old Greek sense of *khronos* or ripeness—made *The American Cause* an extremely compelling book. Shortly after the tragedy Jeffrey Nelson, Russell Kirk's son-in-law and the publisher of ISI Books, proposed that we meet. We did so over dinner in East Lansing on November 5, 2001. Given the response to the attacks on America, marked by a spontaneous outpouring of love of country, Jeff sensed that college students and many others as well would be receptive to Kirk's spirited defense of American civilization in *The American Cause*. I agreed and was honored that he asked me to edit the dated material in earlier editions of this work, which is a short but stirring explication of fundamental American beliefs. At the core of *The American Cause* is a primer on the principles that underlie our nation's government, economy, and civil society. Kirk's explication of these principles, although written almost half a century ago, has never been more timely.

So for the opportunity to work on *The American Cause*, many thanks to Annette Kirk and to Jeffrey Nelson and to the Russell Kirk Center for Cultural Renewal that they established and direct.

I also wish to thank several other individuals who have been helpful. Michigan Governor John Engler, who used to represent the Kirks in the Michigan Senate, sent pertinent essays and articles my way. Bradley Birzer of Hillsdale College made helpful suggestions for the bibliography, and Winston Elliot of the Free Enterprise Institute gave me a forum to test the ideas in the afterword. Kirsten Lietz, librarian with the State of Michigan, helped track down review articles. And my wife Louise, always gracious under a regime of deadlines, fostered a home environment in which I could write; even more heroically, she listened to me read and reread passages from the book. Would that every writer could be blessed with a wife like my Louise!

It goes without saying: for whatever excellence can be found in my work, I am indebted to many. *Ubi veritas, Deus ibi est.*

Gleaves Whitney
East Lansing, Michigan, February 28, 2002

Contents

Editor's Introduction

America is a great nation. But is it an exceptional nation? Does it have a unique mission in human history? Russell Kirk believed so, and nowhere in his early career did he make the case better than in *The American Cause*.[1]

How this enduring primer on American civilization came about is a story in its own right. The book was not originally Kirk's idea. In 1956, he was approached by his friend and publisher Henry Regnery, who urged him to write an elementary statement of the moral, political, social, and economic principles upon which the United States was founded. The Cold War was heating up, and militant Communism was America's mortal enemy. It was crucial that Americans understand what their country stood for, how it differed from the enemy, and why it was worth defending.

Kirk, 37 years old at the time, was at first reluctant to write the primer. He was working on larger projects that had grown out of his magnum opus, *The Conservative Mind*.[2] Regnery's publication of that book just three years earlier had opened up the "intellectual commons" to Kirk. He believed his energies could be better channeled into other book projects. He changed his mind, however, once certain disturbing facts came to light.

What Kirk learned was that many American troops who had been taken prisoner during the Korean War (1950–53) had been easy targets of Communist indoctrination. In fact, the chief of intelligence of the "Chinese People's Volunteer Army" in North Korea had written a memorandum to his superiors in Beijing in which he fairly gloated. "Based upon our observations of American soldiers and their officers captured in this war," this intelligence officer wrote, "the following facts are evidenced." Among other things, "There is little knowledge or understanding, even among United States university graduates, of American political history and philosophy; of federal, state, and community organizations; of states rights and civil rights; of safeguards to freedom; and of how these things supposedly operate within [their] own system."[3]

Americans were justifiably skeptical of an enemy's report—but were later disturbed to learn that it contained more than a grain of truth. Investigation of our troops' conduct and morale in prisoner-of-war camps yielded disturbing insights.[4] A number of our soldiers were indeed ignorant of their own cause. Some had "weak loyalties" to their faith and to their nation. Some had succumbed to Communist propaganda in the absence of torture and without serious resistance. How could this have happened? A Senate subcommittee ventured that American institutions as a whole—not just the public schools—had failed to inculcate the knowledge and values needed for U.S. citizens to defend their nation adequately. One American officer put the matter bluntly: "This is a commentary on manners and morals; on character and lack of it; on a disease that might well be considered the Number One Social Disease of America. Its prevention and its treatment are essential to the continuing survival of our system."[5]

Kirk, himself a soldier during the Second World War, was also disturbed by these findings. He accepted Regnery's commission and in short order produced a 39,000-word manuscript in ten chapters. In 1957 Regnery printed 5,000 copies of the book. It sold for $3.50, and a number of copies were purchased by the U.S. government to distribute to the armed forces.[6] One reviewer wrote that the book would appeal not just to military men but to a broad spectrum of Americans—if they were not ideologues. If you are not an ideologue, Paul Kiniery ventured, "you will like this book which puts into hard-hitting words many of your thoughts and convictions about the gift that is represented by life in the United States."[7]

Regnery went through the initial print run. Within a decade, however, the United States found itself entangled in a new war in Asia. Communism still posed a significant threat to the United States, to be sure. But more serious challenges were arising within the nation. It was the tumultuous Sixties, and the stakes seemed higher. Among college students especially, the essential goodness of the American cause came under serious attack. At the same time, there was little evidence that American institutions had become any more successful at instilling the knowledge and values needed for the nation to fight for its principles and promise. Regnery decided to reprint *The American Cause* in 1966, this time with a foreword by John Dos Passos. Mincing no words, Dos Passos wrote, "It is an appalling thought that *The American Cause* should be more needed today than it was needed on the day it was published nearly ten years ago." But the nation was confronted by a new outbreak of "distemper." Dos Passos hoped that the work would enjoy a wide circulation. He hoped that even student radicals would read *The American Cause* and be inspired by it. "Intelligent radicals," after all, should "find aid and comfort in the principles on which the American republic was founded."[8]

These two early editions of *The American Cause* were met by quite different generations. The book's first readers were members of a generation that in youth had some memory of economic depression, world war, and Cold War. The next wave of readers might as well have been from another planet, so different were the Sixties from the Fifties. They were members of a generation that in youth caused or experienced profound cultural changes, and they were deeply skeptical of American ideas and institutions—indeed, skeptical of America itself.

Since the 1966 edition, new generations of college students have grown up among us. Once again *The American Cause* makes its appearance. And once again, the passage of time reveals the book to be much more than a period piece. It is not just a product of the Fifties, for Kirk focused on the principles underlying American civilization rather than on ephemeral policy debates. It seems especially to speak to Americans in the aftermath of September 11th. Citizens are once again discovering their love of country, and there is a keen desire among Americans to understand our heritage as a self-governing people under the rule of law.

Despite the interest of the Pentagon in *The American Cause*, it is not a government publication. Despite its friendly reception among conservatives, it is not a party manifesto. To approach the book so narrowly is to do Kirk a great injustice. As Dos Passos put it, *The American Cause* is the attempt of one man of letters "to jot down in simple terms a few of the principles upon which American government is based."[9] It endures because of the clarity with which Kirk saw timeless ideas intersecting American history.

Although Kirk believed that the United States was an exceptional nation, he was no jingoist, nor was his book chauvinistic. Kirk had long acknowledged that the nation had "grave faults."[10] Nevertheless, he believed that America was worth vigorously defending, no less in the arena of debate than on the field of battle. Thus, his purpose in writing *The American Cause*, he said, was to offer "a statement of the moral and social principles which the American nation upholds in our time of troubles."

Faced with the findings of the armed forces and U.S. Senate, Kirk was frustrated by the fact that most Americans were "badly prepared for their task of defending their own convictions and interests and institutions against the grim threat" of our nation's enemies. "And in our age, when all civilization is immediately menaced," he warned, "good-natured ignorance is a luxury none of us can afford."[11] Kirk wrote this passage during the Cold War, and he was referring to the armed, militant Communists who threatened the West. But his words are just as apt today, when al-Qaeda and other terrorists menace numerous nations— and the United States above all.

One book that influenced Kirk's thinking about the United States—especially regarding the question of America's national purpose—appeared almost a century before *The American Cause*. It is Orestes Brownson's *American Republic*.[12] Kirk held Brownson in great esteem and called his book "one of the more penetrating treatises on American political theory."[13] Except for their discussion of constitutional principles, there is not much overlap between these two books. They were, after all, composed in quite different centuries and in considerably differing circumstances.

Despite differences in milieu, scope, and audience, *The American Cause* and *The American Republic* are animated by the same idea. As Brownson expressed it, every great nation has "its special work, mission, or destiny." In fact, every people is, "in some sense, a chosen people." He explained: "The Jews were the chosen people of God, through whom the primitive traditions were to be preserved in their purity and integrity, and the Messiah was to come. The Greeks were the chosen people of God, for the development and realization of the beautiful or the divine splendor in art, and of the true in science and philosophy; and the Romans, for the development of the state, law, and jurisprudence."

The United States was also a great nation with a great mission. Brownson wrote that America "has a mission, and is chosen of God for the realization of a great idea. It has been chosen not only to continue the work assigned to Greece and Rome, but to accomplish a greater work than was assigned to either. In art, it will prove false to its mission if it does not rival Greece; and in science and philosophy, if it does not surpass it. In the state, in law, in jurisprudence, it must continue and surpass Rome. Its idea is liberty, indeed, but liberty with law, and law with liberty . . . which secures at once the authority of the public and the freedom of the individual—the sovereignty of the people without social despotism, and individual freedom without anarchy."[14]

What Brownson was saying is that the United States had achieved something unprecedented in human history. Its great contribution was to show the nations how to reconcile justice, order, and liberty. America was the champion, not just of freedom, but of a justly ordered freedom. America's Founders, in other words, had largely got freedom right. They understood that if freedom is not justly ordered, it degenerates either into tyranny or into anarchy. The obligation of succeeding generations of Americans is to continue to get freedom right.

Kirk believed this, too—strongly believed it. In a later essay he wrote, "The American Mission, I maintain with Brownson, is to reconcile the claims of order with the claims of freedom." And—this point is crucial—the American mission is "to maintain in an age of ferocious ideologies and fantastic schemes a model of justice."[15]

Kirk was no chauvinist. On the contrary, readers expecting to find in the conservative Kirk a militant assertion of the "American way" abroad will be disappointed. He appreciated the marvelous variety of human cultures. He eschewed demonizing the foreign. He proposed in *The American Cause* "to steer clear of 'devil terms' and 'god terms.' We shall not argue that a thing is good simply because it is American, or bad simply because it is not American; our endeavor will be to describe the essence of American belief and practice, without preaching a crusade for Americanism."

Kirk explained that *The American Cause* "is not written to convert Americans into political fanatics, zealous for a vague 'Americanism' to be extended over the whole world. Nor is this book written as a piece of propaganda to persuade other peoples that everything American is perfect. One of the most important and beneficial aspects of our American tradition, indeed, is toleration: and this toleration extends to a sympathetic approval of variety, national and private rights, and freedom of choice, both at home and throughout the world. The American mission is not to make all the world one America, but rather to maintain America as a fortress of principle and in some respects as an example to other nations. The American cause is not to stamp out of existence all rivals, but simply to keep alive the principles and institutions which have made the American nation great."[16]

What threatened the American mission, according to Kirk?

The ideologue. Kirk defined the ideologue as one who "thinks of politics as a revolutionary instrument for transforming society and even transforming human nature." Unleashed during the most radical phase of the French Revolution, the spirit of ideology has metastasized over the past two centuries, wreaking horrors. Jacobinism, Anarchism, Marxism, Leninism, Fascism, Stalinism, Nazism, Maoism—all shared the fatal attraction to "political messianism"; all were "inverted religions." Each of these ideologies preached a dogmatic approach to politics, economics, and culture. Each in its own way endeavored "to substitute secular goals and doctrines for religious goals and doctrines." Thus did the ideologue promise "salvation in this world, hotly declaring that there exists no other realm of being."[17]

One of the worst traits of ideology is that its true believers eschew political compromise. They are contemptuous of the politics of prudence. Yet compromise and prudence are two virtues that have been essential to the American achievement from the early days of the Republic. Indeed, compromise and prudence were virtues inherited from the British, who gave shape to colonial Americans' early political experience.

Kirk was not alone in worrying about the threat of ideology to the West. Other twentieth-century thinkers warned of its menace: Raymond Aron, J. L. Talmon, Kenneth Minogue, Eric Voegelin, Gerhart Niemeyer, and Daniel Bell among them. Early in the century, Max Weber, in his famous essay "Politics as a Vocation," observed that two fundamentally different political approaches characterize modernity. One embraces the "ethic of responsibility," the other the "ethic of ultimate ends."

The former understands that politics is the art of the possible, so compromise among competing factions is necessary for the health of the body politic. Those who embrace the ethic of responsibility are respectful of political traditions and inherited customs. They do not think compromise is "dirty." They avoid the hubris of thinking that they and they alone know how all of life should be ordered. They adapt to a pluralistic array of people, beliefs, and factions, and accept pragmatic compromise as necessary to a tolerable order.

By contrast, those who embrace the ethic of ultimate ends disdain such compromise, believing no price too high to achieve their objectives, even if it means the murder of innocent human beings. After all, in a moral crusade, the end justifies *any* means. "One's stainless standard must mow the enemy down."[18]

The ideologues that have plagued the United States in the

past are well known—they are the anarchist who assassinated a president, the Fascists and Nazis who plunged the U.S. into world war, and the Communists who declared, "We will bury you," among many others. However, the United States has, by and large, successfully withstood each successive wave of ideological fanaticism. With the end of the Cold War in the 1990s, it may have seemed for a brief moment in time that the "end of history" had arrived; that the world might now live under a *Pax Americana.*

It was not to be. September 11th abruptly destroyed the illusion that history had ended or that ideology was dead. Al-Qaeda terrorists cut short the nascent *Pax Americana.* Their barbaric acts had all the marks of armed ideology. But instead of marching under the swastika or hammer and sickle, they war under the Crescent, which introduces an interesting twist. For in our day the armed ideologues are not *secular* totalitarians, but *religious* totalitarians—to wit, Islamic extremists.

The vast majority of Americans have traditionally rejected the way of religious totalitarianism. As Kirk persuasively argues in the following pages:

> [T]he religious foundation of our nation, accompanied by complete toleration of legitimate worship and private conscience, does not, of course, mean that we endure religious fanaticism in action, or that we refuse to prosecute

acts which we consider immoral or harmful to society merely because they are committed under the name of religion. When a religious sect or a private believer actively violates the laws of the land, we do not hesitate to take stern steps to restrain such people. But in America any man can hold such religious views, or irreligious views, as he chooses, so long as he does not attempt to force those views upon others and so long as in his actions he does not violate the law.

This combination of complete toleration of opinion with national attachment to religious principle is very rare in the world. Most nations either recognize—formally or implicitly—a state religion, or else disavow religious truth altogether. Such a harmony between church and state is one of the principal achievements of American society, and no powerful religious body in America desires to alter this situation. Americans, then, may take pride in being the most tolerant of people—tolerant without sacrifice of religious conviction.[19]

The foe we must face today is of a different stripe than the one we faced fifty years ago—but not much different. Kirk's words steel us for the battle just as much as if our enemies were the Nazis or Soviets of old.

In editing *The American Cause*, my aim has been to leave Kirk's essay as undisturbed as possible. In a few passages I delete or abbreviate the discussion of Communists as the enemy. But much of Kirk's extensive treatment of the Communist threat in chapters 9 and 10 remains of permanent value when understood in the context of his deeper concern about the destructiveness of nearly every revolutionary movement. In such passages, I change the mention of a specific revolutionary or ideological movement to language reflecting this more universal concern—hence "revolutionary," "revolutionary movement," "ideologue," or "ideological." These modest changes are, I believe, in the spirit of Kirk's original intent.

Reading *The American Cause* anew, I am struck by how Kirk's words retain their grace and conviction, their power and hope. They speak to us in the face of international terror, just as they spoke to our parents in the face of nuclear annihilation. For the bedrock principles upon which America was established live on.

[1] The first edition is Russell Kirk, *The American Cause* (Chicago: Henry Regnery, 1957). The second edition is Russell Kirk, *The American Cause*, Foreword by John Dos Passos (Chicago: Henry Regnery, 1966). Unless otherwise indicated, all citations of *The American Cause* are from the 1966 edition.

[2] The first edition is Russell Kirk, *The Conservative Mind: From Burke to Santayana* (Chicago: Henry Regnery, 1953).

[3] Memorandum quoted in Kirk, *American Cause*, p. 2.

[4] At the time Kirk wrote *The American Cause*, the evidence was collected at Maxwell Field, Alabama, and at Harvard University. Kirk also referenced the Army booklet, "Communist Interrogation, Indoctrination, and Exploitation of Prisoners of War." In addition he cited the published memoirs of several officers and soldiers. See Kirk, *American Cause*, p. 3.

[5] Quoted in Kirk, *American Cause*, p. 3.

[6] Editor interview with Annette Kirk, February 28, 2002.

[7] Paul Kiniery, book review, *Catholic World*, 187 (April 1958): 74.

[8] Dos Passos, foreword to *American Cause*, pp. v, xv. Of relevance is that a student competition sponsored by an organization called Constructive Action, Inc., was included in the republication of the book. See Kirk, *American Cause* (1966 ed.), pp. 153–54.

[9] Dos Passos, foreword to *American Cause*, p. v.

[10] Russell Kirk, *The Conservative Mind: From Burke to Eliot*, 7th ed. (Chicago: Regnery Books, 1986), p. 72.

[11] Kirk, *American Cause*, this edition, p. 1.

[12] Orestes A. Brownson, *The American Republic: Its Constitution, Tendencies, and Destiny* (New York: O'Shea, 1866). A new edition of this work is being published by ISI Books in fall 2002 and contains a substantial introduction by the political philosopher Peter A. Lawler. Much of Brownson's *The American Republic* is a rewriting of Brownson's much earlier essay series on the "Origin and Constitution of Government," published originally in the 1840s in the *Boston Quarterly Review* and *U.S. Democratic Review*.

[13] Kirk, *Conservative Mind*, p. 249.

[14] Brownson, *American Republic*, Introduction, pp. 2-3.

[15] Russell Kirk, "The American Mission," in *Redeeming the Time* (Wilmington, Del.: ISI Books, 1996), p. 180.

[16] Kirk, *American Cause*, this edition, p. 12.

[17] Russell Kirk, "The Errors of Ideology," in *The Politics of Prudence* (Bryn Mawr, Pa.: Intercollegiate Studies Institute, 1993), pp. 1, 5.

[18] See Max Weber, in *From Max Weber: Essays in Sociology*, ed. C. Wright Mills, trans. Hans H. Gerth (Oxford: Oxford University Press, 1946), pp. 77-128; and Daniel Bell, *The End of Ideology: On the Exhaustion of Political Ideas in the Fifties* (Cambridge: Harvard University Press, 1988), ch. 13.

[19] Kirk, *American Cause*, this edition, pp. 37-38.

⇜ Chapter One ⇝

IGNORANCE—
A DANGEROUS LUXURY

This little book is a statement of the moral and social principles that the American nation upholds in our time of troubles. It is not a collection of slogans, nor yet a history of American politics. Intended to be an honest description of the beliefs we Americans live by, *The American Cause* is a brief effort to refresh Americans' minds.

Many Americans are badly prepared for their task of defending their own convictions and interests and institutions against the grim threat of armed ideology. The propaganda of radical ideologues sometimes confuses and weakens the will of well-intentioned Americans who lack any clear understanding of their own nation's first principles. And in our age, good-natured ignorance is a luxury none of us can afford.

THE MEANING OF IDEOLOGY

Our book is intended for the general reader. We try not to take sides concerning religious and political questions which are in dispute in America, but endeavor to state as simply as we can those great convictions upon which nearly all Americans seem to be agreed: to which most Americans agree, by their daily acceptance of these principles as rules of life and politics, even if they themselves cannot easily put their convictions into words. This book does not provide an American "ideology." The word ideology means political fanaticism, a body of beliefs alleged to point the way to a perfect society. Most Americans, this author included, are not political fanatics. But this book does provide, we trust, a concise statement of the beliefs that secure our order, our justice, and our freedom.

When, in the Second World War, our troops landed in North Africa, the French were astonished at how politically naïve American soldiers seemed. For most Frenchmen are passionately interested in political notions; while most Americans— like most English people—are not. This lack of interest in abstract politics is not always a harmful thing. One reason that the Americans, like the English, do not spend much time arguing over theories of politics is that for a very great while nearly all of us have been contented with our society and our form of government. We have not been revolutionaries since 1776 because we have felt that we have enjoyed as good a society as any people reasonably can hope for.

But nowadays, if we mean to defend against our enemies all the good things in our society, we need to study and to think. We are terribly threatened by relentless opponents. We do not need to invent some new theory of human nature and politics; but we do need, urgently, to recall to our minds the sound convictions that have sustained our civilization and our nation. Our enemies, no matter what resources they may have, cannot defeat us if we are strong in our own principles. But if we seem to the rest of the world to stand for nothing; and if we ourselves are ignorant of those ideas and institutions which nurture our culture and our political liberty—why, then we will fall, no matter how great our industrial productivity is, and no matter how many divisions we equip, and no matter what ingenious new weapons we devise.

Fanatic ideologues in our time have drawn their strength from faith in their ideas, evil though most of their ideas have been. When revolutionaries willing to lay down their life for their movement have more faith in their ideology than we have in our ancient principles, and when anti-American ideologues on college campuses can bewilder even American university students by their arguments, then our American cause is in peril.

IDEOLOGY AND IGNORANCE

It is doubtful whether the great majority of American citizens are possessed of any clear understanding of those differences of principle which distinguish their society from that of their adversaries. And this is a perilous condition. There is small danger that the majority of Americans ever will embrace a radical anti-American ideology actively. But there is considerable danger that the majority of Americans may fail to oppose such movements intelligently. It is not required that radical doctrines be accepted with enthusiasm; rather, such nostrums flourish upon the indifference and ignorance of the majority.

We need badly some millions more of Americans who are hard to beat. Our immediate task, it seems, is to re-affirm the faith that has been our nation's. Nowadays we Americans—as Edmund Burke said of Englishmen in the time of the French Revolution—"are combating an armed doctrine." Not so long ago, the armed and fierce doctrine against which we fought was Soviet Communism; before that, it was Nazism; now, it may be some fresh fanatic challenge to the things we love. Our American principles, we think, will stand the test of such a ferocious assault—if only we know those principles. A fanatic armed doctrine can be resisted only by a strong body of sound principles.

Demosthenes, the great Athenian patriot, cried out to his countrymen when they seemed too confused and divided to stand against the tyranny of Macedonia: "In God's name, I beg of you to think." For a long while, most Athenians ridiculed Demosthenes' entreaty: Macedonia was a great way distant, and there was plenty of time. Only at the eleventh hour did the Athenians perceive the truth of his exhortations. And that eleventh hour was too late. So it may be with Americans today. If we are too indolent to think, we might as well surrender to our enemies tomorrow. This small book, despite all its limitations, possibly may encourage some thought.

⇥ Chapter Two ⇤

THE NEED FOR PRINCIPLES

THE AMERICAN CAST OF MIND

Most Americans do not wish to turn the world upside down. By and large, the American people have shown a conservative cast of mind ever since they achieved their independence. Struggle among classes rarely has been fierce in the United States; Americans have been content with their domestic pattern of life and politics. And, except for a few brief interludes, we have intervened in the affairs of other states only reluctantly; we have built no great American empire, and have not attempted to impose American patterns of life and forms of government upon the rest of the world.

For a great power—today the greatest of the powers—the United States has been an astonishingly tranquil and unbelligerent nation. We have known only one violent internal conflict, the Civil War, and that more than a century ago. We have prospered exceedingly in a material way. We have maintained a degree of order and justice and freedom very rare in history. And behind these outward marks of success lie certain enduring principles of thought and action which, in very considerable part, have created and protected our national life. Certain concepts in Americans' minds are responsible for our private rights, our sound government, and our worldly prosperity.

Though most men and women, in any age and any country, live almost unaware that they are governed by certain general ideas, nevertheless nearly everything we have is produced and sheltered by the moral and intellectual assumptions that people take for granted. One cannot see or feel or taste or hear ideas; yet without the existence of great ideas, human beings would be only animals, and could exist only as animals live. Only mankind possesses ideas. The success or failure of any human society depends upon how sound and true its ideas are. That a nation has prospered a great while—that it has been orderly and free and just and wealthy—is one very good proof that its ideas have been sound and true.

Three Bodies of Principle Controlling Any People

At least three groups of ideas, or bodies of principle, invisibly control any people, whether those people are Australian bushmen or highly civilized modern nations. The first, and most important, of these bodies of principle is the set of moral convictions which a people hold: their ideas about the relationship between God and man, about virtue and vice, honesty and dishonesty, honor and dishonor. The second of these bodies of principle is the set of political convictions which a people hold:

their ideas about justice and injustice, freedom and tyranny, personal rights and power, and the whole complex problem of living together peaceably. The third of these bodies of principle is the set of economic convictions which a people hold: their ideas about wealth and property, public and private responsibilities in the affair of making a living, and the distribution of goods and services.

Out of the development of these bodies of principle there grows what we call civilization; and when these bodies of principle are weakened, and a people lose faith in the ideas by which they live, civilization decays. When these bodies of principle are increasing in strength and richness, we say a people are progressive; but when these bodies of principle are decaying in their influence upon men and women, we call such a people decadent. It is by the healthiness of our principles that we measure the success or failure of any society.

These bodies of principle have come into existence among us by a long and mysterious process. Only man recognizes principles, and only man knows civilization. These principles have been built up over a great many centuries, most of them; they are the accumulated accomplishment of countless generations of human beings. We do not know how or when most of them first were recognized by men. Occasionally, in the procession of history, a man of genius contributes something new to these principles, or revives and improves some principle long neglected. But for the most part these ideas are the product of innumerable thinking and working men and women, who come to agree that a particular concept is true. By an age-long process of trial and error—straining people's notions through the sieve of history— some human beliefs are found to be sound and enduring, while others are found to be erroneous and obsolete. Yet a number of human convictions have persisted ever since civilization began, little changed by the passage of time; these seem to be permanent truths, which any civilized nation must reckon with or else decay.

Most Americans are convinced that certain of these enduring truths were revealed to humankind by God: among these principles are the necessity for worshipping the Creator, the essence of private morality, and the nature of love which teaches us our duties toward other men and women. The powers and the limits of human nature, Americans have felt, have been implanted in our minds by divine revelation.

But the majority of the principles by which we live, Americans generally seem to agree, are the product of human experience through the ages, as man struggled up from savagery toward civilization: now making progress, now slipping into decadence. Our convictions about the administration of justice, for instance, and the better patterns of government, and the proper functioning of the economy, are derived from the "wisdom of the species," the trial-and-error lessons of history—though, it should be added, even our system of justice, our forms of law and order, and our economic ways seem to most Americans to be our imperfect human attempts to reproduce in society certain natural laws for human conduct that a divine intelligence decreed.

ORIGIN OF OUR MORAL, POLITICAL, AND ECONOMIC IDEAS

Now these general principles to which most Americans are attached are not themselves—with a very few exceptions—of purely American origin. Our religious and moral convictions had their origin in the experience and thought of the ancient Jews and Greeks and Romans. Our political ideas, for the greater part, are derived from Greek and Roman and medieval European and especially English practice and philosophy. Our economic concepts, some of them, can be traced back to the age of Aristotle and beyond; and even the more recent of these economic ideas were first expressed in eighteenth-century Britain and France, rather than in America. American civilization does not stand by itself: it is part of a great chain of culture which we sometimes call "Western civilization," or "Christian civilization," yet which in some particulars is older even than the culture of Western Europe or the history of Christianity.

Americans, nevertheless, have adapted these ancient principles to the circumstances of life in their country, and often have improved the practical application of these ideas to the workaday world. The Americans, like the Romans, have been conspicuously a people of practical talents. Sometimes they have been so much occupied with practical matters that they have almost forgotten how everything practical really is the application of a general principle. Yet even our immense industrial and techno-logical achievements are possible only through the application of certain scientific theories to achieve material results. The more civilized people become, the more do they depend upon general ideas. Only the primitive savage manages to get along, after a fashion, in a "practical" way, without much reference to moral and intellectual concepts. (But even the savage recog-nizes and obeys some general ideas, if expressed only as taboos and ancient customs.) The savage remains a savage if he does not acquire general principles about which to form his life. The civilized man sinks back into savagery when he forgets the principles that have made possible his material accomplish-ments.

We cannot understand our American cause, therefore, un-less we first understand the principles upon which the American people have formed their complex society. In the chapters that follow, we shall look at the moral convictions of Americans, and see how these moral convictions have been expressed in our na-tional life. We shall look at the political convictions of Ameri-cans, and see how these political convictions have shaped the American government. We shall look at the economic convic-tions of Americans, and see how these economic convictions have accounted for the growth of American industry and commerce. These chapters, in short, will combine a description of Ameri-cans' opinions with a brief account of American institutions. The American cause, the purpose and duty and mission of the United

States in the contemporary world, has grown out of these bodies of principle and out of the practical American experience in the application of these principles. The American, as a type, is not a visionary, a dreamer: he acts upon long-established principles that have been confirmed as valid by the American historical experience. And the American cause is not some vague aspiration toward turning the world upside down, but a sober and prudent defense of beliefs and rights and institutions—the legacy of civilization—which today are threatened by violent and disastrous forces that would destroy not just our citizens but also our culture.

PRINCIPLES AND CIVILIZATION

A man without principles is an unprincipled man. A nation without principles is an uncivilized nation. If a people forget their principles, they relapse into barbarism and savagery. If a people reject sound principles for false principles, they become a nation of fanatics. The thinking American nowadays has to defend sound principle on two fronts: one, the neglect of all principle, which leads to social and personal decadence; the other, the adoption of false principles, which plunges the world into anarchy.

Our danger at home is that a great part of the American people may forget that enduring principles exist. Our danger abroad is that the false principles of revolutionary fanaticism may gain such an influence as to wound us terribly.

The American cause, then, is the defense of the principles of a true civilization. This defense is conducted by renewing people's consciousness of true moral and political and economic principle, and by applying true principle to the institutions of society and private life.

AMERICANISM AND AMERICAN BELIEF

So this book is not written to convert Americans into political fanatics, zealous for a vague "Americanism" to be extended over the whole world. Nor is this book written as a piece of propaganda to persuade other peoples that everything American is perfect. One of the most important and beneficial aspects of our American tradition, indeed, is toleration: and this toleration extends to a sympathetic approval of variety, national and private rights, and freedom of choice, both at home and throughout the world. The American mission is not to make all the world one America, but rather to maintain America as a fortress of principle and in some respects an example to other nations. The American cause is not to stamp out of existence all rivals, but simply to keep alive the principles and institutions which have made the American nation great.

We propose, in this book, to steer clear of "devil terms" and "god terms." We shall not argue that a thing is good simply because it is American, or bad simply because it is not American; our endeavor will be to describe the essence of American belief and practice, without preaching a crusade for Americanism. We shall try to remain free of slogans and clichés. We are not going to oppose an abstract "democracy" to an abstract "absolutism" or "imperialism." Thinking in slogans ends with thinking in bullets. When we speak of democracy, we shall speak of democratic institutions in the United States, not of some misty political ideal that Americans are expected to impose on the universe. When we speak of economic free enterprise, we shall speak of economic practices and developments in the United States, not of some Utopia of perfect competition. In much of the world, political discussion has degenerated into a Babel of furious voices, all crying out abstract god-terms and devil-terms that bear small relation to real governments, or real economies, or real men and women. The American cause cannot be explained or served by strident propaganda of that sort. And the American cause is so complex and living a thing, grown out of such an ancient soil, that it cannot be described in single phrases like "democracy" or "equality." On the contrary, the American cause is made up of many moral and political and economic factors, some of them peculiar to America.

CONFUSED FOREIGN IMPRESSIONS OF AMERICA

No cause can be maintained long unless a considerable proportion of a people understand the meaning of that cause. It seems to us that the number of people who truly understand the complexity of the American cause has grown dangerously small. There are many symptoms. Some of our official representatives abroad, and many of our travelers, are unable to explain American things to Europeans and Asians and Africans: sometimes they apologize confusedly for things that need no apology, or belligerently assert that all things American necessarily are better than all things foreign, and that "American know-how" might solve all the problems of humanity. Within the United States, a dismayingly large number of people seem to assume that our order and justice and freedom and prosperity will continue forever, with no need of *their* help; if they think at all about the forces which keep American society vital, they seem to think of the nation's life as a kind of machine, tended by someone in Washington, from which they have an absolute right to benefit but to which they are obliged to contribute nothing.

And among other people, the impression has been gaining strength—encouraged by the deliberate agitation of militant fanatics—that America is a prosperous barbarian nation, swaggering and covetous, engaged in some design to extend its power over the universe. Or, in a different vein, some men and women in other countries think dreamily of the United States as a place of unbounded resources and endless amusements—and are envious accordingly. There is need for reminding the rest of the world that America is not merely an abstraction, a work of nature: for America really is a highly civilized nation whose achievement has been made possible by the union of enduring traditions with private energies and public responsibilities.

This book is a little window opening on the beliefs and customs and history and practices in America that constitute America's claim to civilization and America's source of well-being. We have written it as a work of renewal, of restoration, in a modest way: a reminder that "the dead alone give us energy," that today's policy must be undertaken in the light of yesterday's experience, and that the American cause has become the cause of all high culture.

≈ Chapter Three ≈

Moral Principle: The Nature of Man

The Religious Character of the United States

The United States is a Christian nation.[1] This is a simple statement of fact, not an argument to advance the American cause. With the exception of the five and a half million American Jews, Christians or people strongly influenced by Christian beliefs make up the great majority of our population.[2] Christianity and Judaism, moreover, come from a common origin, share many centuries of common historical experience, and have in part the same body of literature, those books of the Bible which Christians call the Old Testament; and so far as what can be said in this little book about moral and religious principle, the differences between Christian and Jewish belief are minor. Therefore it is possible to write about a body of religious and ethical principle shared by the majority of Americans. This chapter and the one that follows are concerned with the general outlines of these principles, and with how these religious and moral ideas govern life in America.

Civilization grows out of religion: the morals, the politics, the economics, the literature, and the arts of any people all have a religious origin. Every people, no matter how savage or how civilized, have some form of religion: that is, some form of belief in a great supernatural power that influences human destinies. There had been no state in the whole history of the world that did not formally recognize the existence of God, or gods, until the Communists of Soviet Russia and their satellite states disavowed all religion and made atheism the official belief of the nation. But even the Soviets did not succeed in stamping out religious faith in their own territories; indeed, the influence of Christianity was increasing prior to the fall of the Soviet Empire. And even the Communists recognized that a people cannot exist without a body of moral principles. They tried to substitute for Christianity a body of dogmas called "dialectical materialism." As Orestes Brownson pointed out in 1849, and as Arnold Toynbee has also written, communism was really a kind of caricature of Christianity, borrowing certain of its moral affirmations, imitating its dogmas, and even appropriating some of its phrases. This made communism all the more dangerous: for the superficial similarities between Christian morality and the pretended Soviet morality sometimes deluded Americans and people in other free states into thinking that communism had high moral aspirations.

INDISPENSABILITY OF MORAL PRINCIPLES

Whether or not a person is religiously minded, he would be flying in the face of fact if he should argue that the element of religion in a nation's life can safely be ignored. The whole pattern in which we live our lives is formed by certain religious assumptions about the nature of God and the nature of man, even though we may have only a very vague notion of what the doctrines of religion are. The ideas of freedom, private rights, charity, love, duty, and honesty, for instance, all are beliefs religious in origin. These ideals also are discussed and advanced by philosophers, of course; but the original impulse behind them is religious. And in America, it is the Christian religion, some two thousand years old (or much older, when one includes the Jewish source of Christianity) and now worldwide in influence, which intimately affects our actions.

We cannot go deeply into theology in these two short chapters. But we propose to outline here certain essential Christian doctrines that have formed American character and society, and that are at the heart of the American cause. These beliefs are the fatherhood of God; the brotherhood of man; and the dignity of man. From these beliefs have developed Christian convictions as to how we should conduct our lives, how we should treat our fellow human beings, and what makes life worth living.

AWARENESS OF GOD THE FATHER

Christians know that there exists a supernatural power, which we can perceive only dimly with our imperfect senses: a Supreme Being, the creator of heaven and earth, all-powerful. And that Supreme Being, God, made mankind, as He made everything else; but for the human person He has a special regard and a special mission. God created man in His own image. From time to time in history, God has revealed to man His power and His love. Slowly and painfully, an obscure desert people, the tribes of Israel, came to be aware of the nature of God; and through them, an understanding of God's majesty and intentions—so far as these things can be understood at all by mankind—was transmitted to the Christian world. To Moses on Mount Sinai, to prophets and saints, through miracles—and, most important of all to the Christian, through the person of Jesus of Nazareth, the Christ, the Redeemer—God made himself and his commandments known to mankind. In orthodox Christian doctrine, God became flesh in the person of Jesus, and suffered on the cross so that mankind might understand His nature and follow in His steps.

To men and women, God gradually made known His commandments and His intention for the human race. The Decalogue—the Ten Commandments delivered to Moses—commenced the instruction of man in how he must live with himself and with his neighbors. The teachings of the Hebrew prophets added to this body of knowledge of the divine will. And the life of Christ set the example for the conduct of all human life. Since the death of Christ, the meditations and actions of saints, and the reasoning of learned doctors, have added to Christian belief a great literature explanatory of God's nature and man's duty.

ORIGINAL SIN

Ever since the human race came into existence, the duty of men and women has been to strive to grow like unto God, their creator. But the human being, an obstinate and perverse creature, repeatedly refuses or fails to follow in the steps of God. Every nation, every man and woman—even the best of us—commits evil at one time or another; some people spend most of their lives in doing evil. This failure of man to do good, to follow the commandments of God, is called sin; and sin has existed ever since mankind existed: so whether one considers the story of Adam and Eve to be literally true or a great myth (that is, a truth expressed in a story, disguised so as to make that truth the more striking), what the Christian calls Original Sin is simply a statement that men and women always have failed to follow the good consistently. Any reflective person is aware in his own daily life of how he frequently fails to be what he should: of how he is selfish, angry, obstinate, and vicious. We all sin; the difference between us is only a difference of degree.

God being perfect, that imperfection which we call sin is offensive in God's sight. Thus we all are offenders in God's eyes. Yet out of His love, He forgives the humble and contrite heart, and makes it possible for a person who seeks truth and righteousness to come to know Him. Coming to know God is called salvation—being saved from the sins of this world. But deliberate turning away from God is called damnation—depriving one's self of the divine nature, denying one's own kinship with God, and sinking into the subhuman state of sin.

THE WORLD A PLACE OF TRIAL

No person ever comes to know God perfectly in this world of time and space through which all of us pass for a few brief years. And no person, however vicious, ever quite succeeds in ignoring God in this world. Thus the world is a place of moral suffering, a place of trial; we are God's suffering servants, the Christian believes. Perfect happiness never can be attained upon this earth, in time and space as we know them, or in our perishing physical bodies. We are put into this world by God to be tested. Those who struggle to walk in the path God has pointed out may suffer greatly all their lives; but they will be rewarded by God through immortality, which is beyond time and space: what is called Heaven.

Those who reject God's commandments punish themselves, for they exile themselves forever from God's sight; this is called Hell. For this little worldly existence of ours, the Christian be-

lieves, is not our be-all and end-all. Every human being possesses an immortal soul. Through God's infinite grace, and by
compliance with God's decrees, any person may attain through
this world of suffering a peace beyond all understanding, an
immortality which is purged of the sins and flaws of the world
we now know.

SOULS

Every person has a soul, a distinct essence. That soul is pre-
cious to God. Though all sinners, still all of us are the children
of God, and able to experience His love, if we do not turn our
faces away from Him. We all are brothers in sin; but God has
commanded us to be brothers in righteousness also, and to
treat one another as brothers. This the Christian calls kinship
in Christ. Every human being here below is our brother, in a
mystical sense: in the sense that we all are the spiritual sons of
God.

MYSTICAL BROTHERHOOD

Now men are brothers only in this mystical, spiritual kinship in
Christ. In any literal sense, we are not flesh-and-blood brothers,
or even thirty-second cousins. And we are enjoined to treat as
brothers all the millions of our fellow human beings only because
we all have the same spiritual father, God. If there were no God
the Father, there could be no brotherhood of man. If God is
denied, then men and women merely are bitterly competing little

organisms, with no moral obligations to one another. They are not brothers, but fierce rivals.

Human Dignity

This creature called man, who contains a spark of immortal life that is his personality, possesses dignity. That dignity is conferred upon him by God; and without God, there can be no human dignity. By "the dignity of man," Christians mean that every living person is entitled to be treated as a son of God, with respect for his personality. No matter how debauched or hideous or stupid a man may seem, he is entitled to certain rights and privileges, to be treated with a certain dignity, because he *is* a man and therefore a son of God, a brother in Christ. Few of us seem dignified in the ordinary conduct of life; nevertheless, our humanity entitles us all to be treated by our fellows as something better than animals. We have no right to treat our fellow human beings as if they were beasts; we owe even the least lovable of them our mercy and our charity. For there is in every one of them an immortal spirit, which comes from God; and if we treat them with indignity, in some sense we are insulting God.

Natural Rights

From this concept of the dignity of man—a dignity that exists only through our relationship with God—there has grown up a recognition of what are called "natural rights." These are the rights that all men and women are entitled to: rights that belong to them simply because they participate in human dignity. There are other rights in our world: rights conferred by society at large, or by certain political and economic and social groups. These latter are man-made rights. But natural rights are rights that originate in the nature of every person—the character and personality given to all people by God, the privileges that come from the fatherhood of God and the brotherhood of man. Everyone is entitled to possess these rights, no matter how strong or how weak he is, no matter how rich or how poor, no matter how civilized or how savage, no matter how famous or how humble.

Precisely what these rights are never has been entirely agreed upon, even among professed Christians. The medieval philosophers of the Church debated for centuries on the character and extent of these rights: St. Thomas Aquinas's description of the rights of nature is one of the more important. Richard Hooker, an English theologian, discussed natural rights and natural laws in the sixteenth century, and his writings greatly influenced subsequent English and American opinion. John Locke, in the seventeenth century, said that there are three primary natural rights, "life, liberty, and property." In America, Thomas Jefferson, in the Declaration of Independence, made these rights "life, liberty, and the pursuit of happiness." Edmund Burke, perhaps the greatest modern political thinker, when he criticized the confused notions of natural rights then popular among the French revolutionaries, went on to say that there are certain true and abiding natural rights, though they cannot always be set down independently and without qualification. Among them, he wrote, men have a right to live by law, for law is made to benefit them. "Men have a right to live by that rule; they have a right to do justice, as between their fellows, whether their fellows are in public function or in ordinary occupation. They have a right to the fruits of their industry, and to the means of making their industry fruitful. They have a right to the acquisitions of their parents; to the nourishment and improvement of their offspring; to instruction in life, and to consolation in death." But, Burke added, "Men have no right to what is not reasonable, and to what is not for their benefit."

Natural Duties

Generally speaking, Christians seem agreed that every right is joined to a corresponding duty. For every right we receive from God, we have a duty toward God; for every right of ours that others respect, we are bound to respect the rights of others. Natural "rights" are the things that our fellow human beings are forbidden to take away from us, under the laws of God. Every man has the right to charity, if he needs charity; but he also has the duty of laboring as best he can for himself, and of helping others if he can. Every man has the right to life; but he also has the duty of respecting the lives of others. A man may forfeit his natural rights by abuse: thus the thief forfeits the right to charity, and the murderer forfeits the right to life.

These natural rights impose upon all men and women certain limits and duties. We have no right to take another's life except to save our own or others' lives. We have no right to take away another's possessions without his consent, except when he has refused to pay to his neighbor or his community what he justly owes. We have no right to abuse, beat, torture, and debase other human beings, for they have a God-given right to dignity. And we have the great duty declared by Jesus in the Sermon on the Mount: to do unto others as we would have others do unto us.

Thus natural laws and natural rights and natural duties all are part of a divine plan for human destiny. They are the laws and rights and duties that arise from the enduring nature that God has given to human beings. The Christian believes that human nature does not change: the character of man in this world always will be what it is now, to the end of time—a mixture of good and evil. Therefore these natural rights and duties always will endure. It is better for a man to die than to surrender his natural rights or to ignore his natural duties. And this Christian concept of right and duty lies at the foundation of American society and government.

IMPOSSIBILITY OF WORLDLY PERFECTION

Human nature will not change so long as this world endures, the Christian thinks. Good and evil always will be at war in human nature. And as human nature never will be perfected in the mortal world, so human society never will reach perfection this side of eternity. It is our Christian duty in this world always to fight for the right; but we are not to expect that we ever shall succeed in establishing the perfect society or in developing the perfect human. It takes all our energies merely to keep evil in check, or to make modest progress in human affairs from time to time. Perfection exists only beyond space and time, in the kingdom of God: in what is called Heaven.

Thus the destiny of man, as a child of God, will be completed only in a timeless and spaceless realm beyond the limits of our little world. Man is made for eternity. Because of the sins that we inflict upon ourselves, we suffer in this world; but that suffering will be wiped away by an existence in immortality, if we choose to love and obey God. As fleshly creatures, we are not made for perfection; it is only when we "put off mortality" that we can love and understand and share the perfection of God. It is one of the punishments of our sins that we would not love a perfect human nature, or a perfect society, even if we found such things in this little world of ours. Man as we know him, "the average sensual man," is perpetually discontented: he lusts after whatever he seems to lack. Whatever life he is living, the grass always seems greener on the other side. He is naturally envious and rebellious and proud. If ever the average sensual man—or any one of us—found himself, untransformed by death and immortality, in the perfect society, he would set to work at once abolishing that perfect society; for mortal man always is bored with what does not change. If ever the average sensual man—or any of us—found himself, untransformed by death and immortality, confronting the perfect human being, he would envy and perhaps destroy that human perfection. Precisely that was the fate of Jesus Christ, to be slain by those he had come to save. Here on earth, we crucify perfect things.[3] It is only in another world than this that we shall love perfection and become part of it.

Therefore Christianity teaches resignation: not to expect perfection in this world. But it also teaches hope: aspiration to attain immortality and perfection, in another realm, through following the path that God has pointed out. And it reminds men and women that their duty is always to work for their own salvation and for the sake of others, even though no one ever will be perfectly happy in this world of ours.

SUMMARY OF CHRISTIAN DOCTRINE

In essence, then, the Christian faith is this. God exists, a stern judge but a loving father to all mankind. Man has been made in God's own image; but man, an imperfect image of God, torments himself by his tendency to sin. The world is always a battleground between good and evil in human nature. All men are brothers in spirit, because they have a common spiritual father, God; and they are enjoined to treat one another as brothers. Because they are made in the image of God, and are brothers in Christ, they possess human dignity. From this human dignity come rights peculiar to man which no one is morally free to violate. The revelations by God establish the way in which men are to live with one another. Justice and peace and charity all flow from God's commandments, given in a spirit of love. Christ will redeem from sin the man who accepts him as savior. The reward of loving obedience to God is eternal life, perfection beyond this world. The self-punishment of defiant sin is never to know God, and thus to lose immortality. Human nature and society never will become perfect in the course of history. Yet God's love rules the world; and happiness, if we are to find it at all in this life, comes from doing God's will. As the essence of man is more than merely mortal, so the destiny of man is more than merely human. The spirit will survive the flesh, and when the end of all earthly things arrives, those who love God shall find a peace that the mortal world never knows. Men who expect to create a heaven upon earth, in defiance of the laws of man's nature and the revelation of God, can create only hell upon earth.

Such is the Christian creed. Whether one subscribes to this religious faith or not, indisputably this is the religious framework upon which American society is built. Christian morality is the cement of American life; and Christian concepts of natural law, natural rights, and necessary limitations to human ambitions all govern our politics and even our economic system. That all Americans do not always abide by Christian teachings scarcely needs to be confessed. The immediate disciples of

Christ did not always abide by all of Christ's teachings: for human nature is flawed, enslaved periodically or regularly to sin, and if the spirit is willing, still the flesh is weak. Our American society is far from perfect. Yet it is a society that works, and which ensures a tolerable measure of order and justice and freedom to men and women; as human societies go, it is a very high achievement. Our American order and justice and freedom would not be possible at all without the framework of religious and moral principle that we have described in the preceding pages.

THE CARICATURE OF RELIGION

Now this whole body of religious and moral principle came under attack by the revolutionary totalitarians of the twentieth century. The enemies of the American cause dissent radically from the Christian concept of God's nature, human nature, human destiny, natural rights, and the moral rules which govern society. The official doctrine of the Nazis, for instance, repudiated Christianity—although admitting the existence of a Supreme Being, or at least of powers more than human—and rejected those concepts of human dignity and natural rights which are so closely interwoven into our view of life and our society. The horrors of the Nazi concentration camps were justified, in the Nazis' argument, by their denial that men are bound by any Christian moral laws: strength, in the Nazi view, was the only source of morality.

The Communists also repudiated Christian teaching, in some respects even more thoroughly than did the Nazis. They were thoroughgoing atheists, for one thing, substituting an abstract "The People" for God. It is not God's will that must be done, in the Communist ideology, but The People's will. In other respects, however, the Communists' doctrines are perversions of Christian doctrines, and sometimes even seem closely to resemble Christian beliefs. Christianity, for instance, teaches that all men are equal in the sight of God—though in no other way. Communism teaches that even though there is no God, men ought to be equal politically and economically in this world. Christianity also teaches that we owe one another charity, because we are brothers and sisters in Christ. Communism teaches that though Christ was an impostor, no one ought to have more than another, and therefore Communist society will take away possessions from one person and give to another. Christianity, moreover, teaches that after life is over, and the end of all things has come, then those who love God shall attain a heavenly perfection. Communism, for its part, teaches that by revolution and compulsion the perfect society shall be established here on earth, and all men shall be perfectly happy, free to "hunt in the morning," in Marx's words, "fish in the afternoon, make love in the evening, and criticize at dinner just as they please"—a child's dream of pleasure.

But these Communist ideals are a caricature of Christian principles. Cut off from their roots, these shadowy copies of

Christian aspirations have led only to a hell upon earth. Although the Communists have preached brotherhood, in practice they have murdered many millions of innocent people. Although the Communists have praised absolute equality, they have established absolute despotism. Although the Communists have aped Christian charity in words, they have resorted to theft and confiscation in actuality. Although the Communists have promised Utopia, they have delivered whole nations to mortal torment. Although they have talked unendingly of peace, they have thriven by war.

Such is the result of supposing that men will be virtuous and good after they have denied the fatherhood of God and the brotherhood of man. The Christian principles that sustain American society are not always observed in America. But they never are entirely forgotten. They breathe life into our nation; they make us truly human. They are sound principles, sound in describing the nature of God and the nature of man. Behind them is a great weight of authority and tradition and practice. Upon them, even more than upon our political and our economic theories and institutions, rests the American cause.

[1] Editor's note: As is evident by the context of this paragraph, Kirk's concept of the religious character of the U.S. is better conveyed in the more contemporary formulation, "Judeo-Christian." This conceptual framework within Kirk's corpus is more fully developed in his landmark study of Western civilization, *The Roots of American Order* (1974), especially chapter two.

[2] Editor's note: In 1900 the United States was 96 percent Christian. In 1970 it was 90 percent Christian. Today it is 85 percent Christian (defined as households

adhering to some form or denomination of Christianity). Conversely, non-Christians constitute approximately 15 percent of the U.S. population today. Of the 40 million or so non-Christians in the U.S., about 5.5 million are Jewish; about 5.5 million are Muslim; and fewer than 1 million are professed atheists.

[3] Editor's note: In the biblical account of Adam and Eve, this is precisely the point. Before the Fall in the Garden of Eden, the parents of mankind were surrounded by perfection itself, yet they still were not content.

❊ Chapter Four ❊

MORAL PRINCIPLE: CHURCH AND STATE

AMERICAN TOLERATION

Complete toleration of religious belief and freedom of worship prevail throughout the United States. *Toleration* of all religious convictions, and toleration even of disbelief in any religion; but not indifference to religion: such is our national policy. The first clause of the First Amendment to the Constitution of the United States runs, "Congress shall make no law respecting an establishment of religion, or prohibiting the free exercise thereof." This provision originally was binding only upon the federal government, as distinct from the state governments; but nearly all the state constitutions contain similar provisions, and none of the states now has an established church.

AMERICAN CONSTITUTION ON RELIGION

And this first clause of the First Amendment was intended to shelter religion, not to hamper churches. Because from the beginning America's population consisted of Christians of many sects, with a sprinkling of Jews and people of other faiths, it would have been impractical and unjust for Congress to have established any one denomination as the state church. The majority of the framers of the Constitution were Episcopalians, but there were also Congregationalists, Presbyterians, Quakers, Unitarians, Methodists, Baptists, Catholics, and a few Deists—notably Jefferson and Franklin—among the founders of the Republic. Not one of our early statesmen was a professed atheist; and all of our presidents, with the possible exception of Jefferson, have publicly professed faith in Christian doctrines. (Jefferson drew up privately his own version of what he believed to be the direct teachings of Christ, the "Jefferson Bible"; and though unconvinced of the divinity of Jesus, he was profoundly attached to Christian morals.) From the first, then, we have been a Christian nation.

Jefferson once wrote to the Bey of Tunis, a Muslim ruler, that "the United States is not a Christian nation." By this, Jefferson meant that there being no establishment of religion in America, a Mohammedan ruler was not debarred by his own religion from dealing with the United States. In that sense, truly, the American government does not avow any particular religious creed. But, as Justice Joseph Story wrote in 1833 concerning the First Amendment to the Constitution, "The general if not the universal sentiment in America was that Christianity ought to receive encouragement from the state so far as was not incompatible with the private rights of conscience and the freedom of religious worship."

This view was sustained by the federal Supreme Court through the mid-twentieth century. As Justice William O. Douglas wrote in a Supreme Court decision of 1951, "We are a religious people whose institutions presuppose a Supreme Being. We guarantee the freedom to worship as one chooses. We make room for as wide a variety of beliefs and creeds as the spiritual needs of man deem necessary. . . . When the state encourages religious instruction or cooperates with religious authorities by adjusting the schedule of public events to sectarian needs, it follows the best of our traditions."

In many ways, we publicly recognize the authority of religious principle. The sessions of our Congress and our state legislatures open with prayers. We exempt the property of churches from taxation. We exempt ministers of religion from military service. We proclaim national days of prayer and Thanksgiving that are religious in inspiration. We allow various expenditures of public funds for certain purposes friendly to religion. We swear oaths in courts on the Bible. Our official pledge of allegiance to the flag and the Republic now includes the words, "one nation, under God." Many of our oaths of office include acknowledgement of God's sovereignty. As a people, we believe that any just political authority must be consecrated in God's sight.

This sense of the religious foundation of our nation, accompanied by complete toleration of legitimate worship and private conscience, does not, of course, mean that we endure religious fanaticism in action, or that we refuse to prosecute acts which we consider immoral or harmful to society merely because they are committed under the name of religion. When a religious sect or a private believer actively violates the laws of the land, we do not hesitate to take stern steps against such people. But in America people can hold such religious views, or irreligious views, as they choose, so long as they do not attempt to force those views upon others and so long as their actions do not violate the law.

This combination of complete toleration of opinion with national attachment to religious principle is very rare in the world. Most nations either recognize—formally or implicitly—a state religion, or else disavow religious truth altogether. Such a harmony between church and state is one of the principal achievements of American society, and no powerful religious body in America desires to alter this situation. Americans, then, may take pride in being the most tolerant of people—tolerant without sacrifice of religious conviction. We are a Christian nation that observes religious principles in its public acts, though enforcing religious convictions upon no one.

TOLERATION ABROAD

In its dealings with other people, the U.S. government has been scrupulously tolerant of religious beliefs and establishments. When, in 1846 and subsequent years, we occupied the region that is now the southwestern United States—and had been Mexican territory—it was inhabited almost entirely by Roman Catholics; but though Protestantism greatly predominated in the United States, we interfered in no way with Catholicism there; we respected church properties and religious convictions, as earlier we had in our purchase of Louisiana. When we occupied, in 1898, the Philippines, Guam, and other territories formerly Spanish, we were equally tolerant. When we occupied Japan following the Second World War, we left the Buddhist and Shinto temples unmolested. Our troops in Europe were careful never to intervene in religious matters. We have maintained cordial relations with Muslim, Buddhist, Hindu, and even irreligious states and rulers.

This does not mean that as a nation we have been indifferent to religious belief, or hostile toward religious belief, throughout the world. On the contrary, we have quickly extended refuge to fugitives from religious or irreligious persecution; when it has been in our power, we have employed every prudent means to discourage or moderate religious or irreligious fanaticism in other countries. The Nazi persecution of the Jews was one of the principal causes of our eventual declaration of war against Germany, and the Communist persecution of Christians in eastern Europe is a principal reason for our alliances with other nations to restrain the Soviets. There are circumstances under which, undoubtedly, we would fight to defend the religious convictions that we share as Christians and Jews, even though American churches and American material interests might not be immediately involved.

Not Indifferent to Religion

But this does not mean that our diplomacy is governed by preference for one religion over another, or even by a regular hos-
tility toward irreligious governments. Ever since President
Washington's Farewell Address, we Americans have recognized
that it is neither right nor expedient for us to dictate, in politics
or in religion, to the rest of the world. We believe that—except
for extreme cases of persecution which seem to violate the whole
body of natural law—every nation must be left to follow the
dictates of its own religious creed. Powerful though the United
States is today, not even America has the strength—let alone the
wisdom—to sit in judgment upon every theological and moral
question raised in Europe and Asia and Africa. If foreign powers engage in policies that many of us may consider intolerant[1]
or immoral, still we do not feel entitled to act against those
powers unless their policies contravene international agreements
to which we are party, or unless those policies immediately
menace the very foundation of religious and moral order in the
world.

Though we all in a sense, as individuals, are our brothers'
keepers, as a political power the United States has not been appointed the keeper of the world's conscience. The toleration that
we practice at home extends also to our foreign policy. From
month to month, many things are done under the sun that Americans, as a nation, tend to think wrong; but the Republic of the

United States, not caring to become a Don Quixote among the nations, generally does not try to set other nations in the path of righteousness. Great states, like private persons, must seek out their own salvation. As a world power, then, we are not a self-righteous nation; or, at worst, we try not to be.

POSITIVE LAW NOT IDENTICAL WITH MORAL LAW

Simply because an unjust act is committed in the affairs of nations, we are not obliged to try to set matters right; if we tried anything of the sort, we should become international busybodies, and should be disliked as all busybodies are disliked. It is only when our great national interests or the sources of modern civilization are threatened that we feel justified in using our national power to enforce the rules of international law. The observance of moral principles in international affairs, as in private life, must depend principally on voluntary and habitual obedience to the moral order, persuasion, and force of public opinion. Just as we do not and can not station policemen in our homes to make sure that everyone behaves decently, so we do not and can not act, we Americans, as a moral police force zealously watching and admonishing foreign governments. Nationally, we are ruled by Christian principles; but Christian nations, like Christian persons, need frequently to recall the Christian doctrine, "Judge not, that ye be not judged." A Christian is not under the illusion that he can stamp out evil, forever, by using force. And thus a Christian nation that understands its own religion cannot presume to be a permanent censor and regulator of the ways of other states. It would be an un-Christian policy to compel other peoples to behave in what we Americans, at any particular moment, might take to be the Christian way.

There are many international concerns, then, in which Americans—though for the most part Christian in belief—do not presume to enforce obedience to strict Christian morals. This is no less true in our domestic concerns. Since our Republic was founded, we have made few attempts to write Christian dogmas into our statute books. Some fundamental principles of morality, essential both to Christianity and to any decent civil social order, are to be found in the laws of the federal government and of every state, it is true: the prohibitions and penalties concerning murder, assault, robbery, and fraud, for instance. But such laws are common to all civilized people, with the partial exception of certain modern totalitarian states. No decent society could subsist without them; in this sense, all law is the reflection of certain great moral convictions. These fundamentals aside, however, we do not often attempt to regulate by law the complexities of private morality. In America, a man may stay within the law and yet do a considerable number of immoral things. He may lie, seduce, neglect his duties, waste his life, denounce his God, and yet run small risk of ever going to prison. He may be sensual, selfish, envious, and arrogant, and yet never come within the jurisdiction of our courts. He may break several of the Ten Commandments, and yet go scot-free all his life. The law of the state, in short, does not take cognizance of many failings that Christians regard as sinful. We do not try to make our law-code identical with the Christian code of ethics. We restrict the operation of our positive laws to those essential matters of public security that cannot be neglected without immediate danger to the whole fabric of civilized society.

This attitude toward the role of positive law—which we share with Britain and with many European states—is not anti-Christian or un-Christian. It is simply a wise recognition of the fact that if the political authority tries to do everything, it will end by doing nothing well. In most matters of private conduct and personal relationships, the state cannot intervene wisely or successfully; for judges and policemen are only human beings, with limited time and limited intelligence, and they are busy enough already, endeavoring—with only partial success—to enforce the bare essentials of public morality. And no nation can, or should, appoint half its population as judges and policemen to watch and reprimand the other half. Politics, it is said, is the art of the possible. Practical morals, too, is the art of the possible. It simply is not possible for political authority to enforce Christian morality, or any other sort of morality, in the everyday concerns of every man and woman. The regulation of ordinary conduct has to be left to private conscience, the influence of habit, custom, and example, and fear and respect for the opinions of one's neighbors.

By restricting itself to enforcing—as best it can—a few moral principles of general and inescapable concern, a political state does not repudiate Christian teaching. On the contrary, only by such a prudent restraint of its own authority can any just government uphold Christian morality. For a state that should arrogantly try to do what no state can do successfully—which should try to regulate every detail of private conduct on some absolute moral plan—soon would become a thoroughly oppressive state. Even to commence such a course of action, the state would have to employ a crowd of spies, informers, and insufferable inspectors; even to begin to enforce its decrees under this system, the state would have to rely upon an army and a police force greater than even those possessed by Soviet Russia.

Our American laws, then, are a reflection of moral law, and especially of Christian moral belief. But they are not the whole of moral law or of Christian morality. They settle for the possible: for what the political authority can undertake with reasonable efficiency and reasonable regard for private freedom.

So when we hear, within the United States or abroad, superficial reproaches about the American failure to make Christianity work in practical politics, we need make no shamefaced apologies. No nation in all history ever succeeded in making, through the judge and the policeman, its religion or its moral code the inflexible law of the land. When such doctrinaire experiments have been tried, they have been catastrophic failures. All men and women are fallible, even the best of them. All that the law can do, in any country, is to maintain a tolerable balance of order and justice and freedom. The law cannot reconstitute human nature; it can only protect most decent human beings, most of the time, against the minority of indecent human beings. The morals and the laws of the United States, like those of other nations, cannot be fairly measured against some impossible standard of absolute perfection. That perfect justice and perfect morality never have existed among men.

AMERICAN REPUBLIC AND RELIGIOUS TEACHINGS

But measured by any reasonable standard—by the yardstick of history or in the scales of justice—the American Republic has succeeded astonishingly well in applying Christian religious and moral principles to governing. The United States has a government of laws, not of men. Enduring rule—not personal caprice— is the supreme authority. The United States has a regard for charity, honesty, and human dignity unexcelled anywhere in the modern world. The United States has a system of justice founded upon the recognition of a justice more than human. The United States has a working political organization that makes right, not mere expediency, its aspiration. The United States enjoys a measure of toleration, public and private, almost unique in history. The United States has sound security of life and property; regular redress for serious wrongs; and a domestic peace possible only because most Americans continue to believe in the Decalogue, the preachings of the prophets, the teachings of Christ, and the reasonings of the great divines.

In the United States, the depredator generally does not go unpunished, and the unfortunate generally does not go to ruin. No nation has any right to be smug; for every nation's performance always falls short of that nation's duties. Yet, judged comparatively, America has some reason to be proud of her obedience to religious and moral truths. There always is immense room for improvement, anywhere. America's union of religious conviction with practical policy, nevertheless, has been as successful as most marriages can hope to be. Surely the fierce totalitarian regimes of our age have no just claim to say, Pharisee-like, to America, "I am holier than thou."

[1] Editor's note: Religious freedom hardly exists among some of America's important allies, even in nations where U.S. troops are stationed to protect them from outside threats. Consider Saudi Arabia. The U.S. State Department's most recent "International Religious Freedom Report" (October 26, 2001) observes that "Saudi Arabia is an Islamic monarchy without legal protection for freedom of religion, and such protection does not exist in practice." All citizens must be Muslims. The Kingdom's fundamental law is constructed around the Koran and *hadith,* or sayings of the Prophet Mohammed. The government has set up a Committee to Promote Virtue and Prevent Vice. The Mutawwa'in, or religious police, patrol streets in search of violators of Islamic law. Worshippers of other faiths may practice their religion in private, but proselytes risk being lashed, thrown into prison, or deported. Apostasy is not tolerated: conversion of a Muslim to another religion is punishable by death if the accused does not recant.

☙ Chapter Five ❧

POLITICAL PRINCIPLE: ORDERED LIBERTY

FOUNDATIONS OF AMERICAN REPUBLICANISM

The United States of America is a federal republic: a federation of states governed by written constitutions. A part of the American political system is almost peculiar to the United States, particularly the checking and balancing of powers and interests by an elaborate system of enduring laws. But the political theories and customs that support our political institutions are very ancient in origin, most of them, and not peculiar to America.

Our constitution is republican—that is, designed to secure the public good through the sharing of political power among many people. The framers of our federal Constitution had in mind, as a model for American government, the ancient Roman republic, and Roman law and institutions still may be discerned in the structure of our government. And they also had in mind—so much at the back of their minds, indeed, that it formed the basis of most of their political opinions—the political experience of England, and English political philosophy. Thus our American governments had for their foundation the English common law, English constitutional practice, and English political theory; and to their English legacy the founders of our Republic added Roman features.

AMERICAN POLITICS NOT ABSTRACT

Unlike the leaders of the French Revolution, the founders of the American Republic were not abstract theorists. (An acute German observer, Friedrich Gentz, perceived the difference between the American and French experiments at the end of the eighteenth century, and pointed out that while the American Revolution was intended to secure in a practical fashion the American institutions and rights that already existed, the French Revolution was an attempt to turn a nation upside down and create something that never before had existed.) The signers of the Declaration of Independence and the framers of the Constitution did not create a republic out of whole cloth. Liking America much as they found it, they overturned English rule chiefly so that they might simply preserve the justice and order and freedom that the American colonies had long enjoyed. They were not creating Utopia; what they aimed at was the preservation, the conservation, of the rights and benefits they had inherited from their forefathers.

Thus when we speak of the theories that underlie our constitutions here in America, we do not mean a set of abstract doctrines constructed overnight to support some brand-new political system. By American political theories, rather, we mean those assumptions, bound up with certain moral principles, that Americans believe have been tested by many centuries of civilized experience—some of that experience here in America, most of it in Europe. For the most part, American political theories were developed from the combination of the theological and moral principles discussed in preceding chapters with the practical working of the European and English and American civil social order in history. Washington and Hamilton, Adams and Morris, Jefferson and Madison, knew history thoroughly. They were aware of the intricate process by which people had learned to live together in justice and order and freedom. They knew of the many mistakes that states had made, and of old political institutions which had proved themselves beneficial. They were acquainted with the growth of common law and constitutional government in England, and with the experience of colonial Americans in free institutions. Even the more radical among the founders of American government, like Thomas Jefferson, looked steadily to the past for guidance. Realizing that politics is the art of the possible, they settled for sound security in social institutions. They were not closet-philosophers, vainly pursuing the vision of a perfect society independent of human experience.

They knew political philosophy, as well as history and law. They had read, many of them, Plato and Aristotle, Cicero and Seneca, St. Augustine and Dante, Sir Edward Coke and Richard Hooker, John Locke and Edmund Burke. They knew the writings of Kames and Blackstone and other legal theorists. But they were not bookish in the bad sense of that word: they did not divorce theory from practice. In their own careers they had united the authority of social custom with the authority of great books. They respected the wisdom of their ancestors. Especially they respected religious wisdom: nearly all of them had been brought up on the King James Version of the Bible, and most of them were intimately acquainted with the English Book of Common Prayer. Thus their political assumptions were compounded of Jewish religious doctrines, Christian teachings, classical philosophy, medieval learning, and English literature. And they were accustomed to testing these assumptions by reference to the historical experience of the ancient world, medieval society, English social development, and the American colonial experience. Out of such materials came the framework of our American Republic. We are a modern nation only in a restricted sense.

THREE CARDINAL IDEAS OF WESTERN POLITICS

Now in the political beliefs of what we call "Christian civilization" or "Western civilization"—of which American civilization is a part—there are three cardinal ideas: the idea of justice, the idea of order, and the idea of freedom. These three great concepts are the cement of American society. These three ideas dominated the minds of the founders of our Republic, and they are the principles that underlie American politics nowadays. These concepts of justice and order and freedom have been derived from Jewish and classical and Christian and European thought and experience. They are not peculiarly American; but they are essential to American social existence, and they have attained a high degree of practical expression in American life. They make possible the ordered liberty that is among the chief justifications of the American cause.

"Justice" is the principle and the process by which each man is accorded the things that are his own—the things that belong to his nature. This concept the old Greeks and Romans expressed in the phrase "to each his own."[1] It is the principle and the process that protects a man's life, his property, his proven rights, his station in life, his dignity. It also is the principle and the process that metes out punishment to the evil-doer, which enforces penalties against violence and fraud. The allegorical figure of Justice always holds a sword. Justice is the cornerstone of the world—divine justice and human justice. It is the first necessity of any decent society.

"Order" is the principle and the process by which the peace and harmony of society are maintained. It is the arrangement of rights and duties in a state to ensure that a people will have just leaders, loyal citizens, and public tranquility. It implies the obedience of a nation to the laws of God, and the obedience of individuals to just authority. Without order, justice rarely can be enforced, and freedom cannot be maintained.

"Freedom" is the principle and the process by which a man is made master of his own life. It implies the right of all members of adult society to make their own choices in most matters. A slave is a person whose actions, in all important respects, are directed by others; a free man is a person who has the right—and the responsibility—of deciding how he is to live with himself and his neighbors.

THE AMERICAN POLITY

Some nations have order without justice or freedom; these we usually call tyrannies. Other nations have freedom—for a while— without justice or order; such conditions we call anarchy. The founders of the American Republic, equally detesting tyranny and anarchy, determined to establish an enduring political constitution that would recognize the claims of justice, order, and freedom, and that would allow no excessive demands upon the part of any one of these three principles. Such a state, in which interests are balanced and harmonized by good laws, Aristotle had called a "polity." Our American polity is a regime of ordered liberty, designed to give justice and order and freedom all their due recognition and part. The founders of the Republic worked prudently with the materials they felt had been given to them by Providence: the American colonial experience of parliamentary government and local rights; the English legacy of common law and checks upon power; the Christian theories of natural law and natural rights; the classical ideal of a republic; and the Old Testament morality that was the fundamental educational discipline of eighteenth-century Americans. They indulged in no political fantasies. The chief philosophical explanations of their aims and methods are *The Federalist Papers,* written by Hamilton, Madison, and Jay, and *A Defence of the Constitutions of Government of the United States,* written by John Adams. Their enduring monument is the Constitution of the United States.

CONTRAST WITH FRENCH REVOLUTION

In the French Revolution, which began fourteen years later than the American Revolution, the revolutionary leaders—at least at the climax of the revolutionary movement—paid little heed to the ancient principles of justice, order, and freedom. They were not Christians; and, though they admired the political forms of Greek and Roman days, they felt no respect for the political traditions of their own country. Little influenced by a reverence for the wisdom of their ancestors, therefore, the chief French revolutionaries set out to establish what they thought would be a completely rational and completely new political order, independent of Providence and historical experience. In place of the old ideals of justice, order, and freedom, they shouted a novel slogan: "Liberty, equality, fraternity!" In their brave new world, the French reformers felt confident, all men would be absolutely free, perfectly equal, and happy in social harmony. The duration of their dream was brief: fierce conspiracies and mass-executions gave the lie to their expected fraternity, a succession of cliques of intolerant politicians undid their expected equality, and the triumph of a dictator, Napoleon, put an end to the anarchic liberty they had celebrated.

Having left Providence and historical experience and prudence out of their considerations, the French reformers passed speedily from the ineffectual monarchy of the Old Regime to the efficient tyranny of the Napoleonic Empire. The coming of Napoleon Bonaparte, indeed, was welcomed by the majority of the French; for though he ended freedom, he restored justice and order. And men cannot be content without justice and order.

The American Republic and its Constitution, in contrast, have endured with some amendment for more than two centuries. This remarkable permanence seems to be the product of the wisdom of the Republic's founders: they built upon the living rocks of justice, order, and freedom. Therefore it is worthwhile to examine what they understood by the terms justice, order, and freedom. By and large, the American cause today rests upon their understanding of the meaning of those great ideas; for, perhaps more than any other people in the modern world, we are devoted to our national political traditions and venerate the documents in which they are expressed.

"TO EACH HIS OWN"

The American revolutionary leaders, and the framers of the Constitution, believed that true justice can be obtained through recognizing the legitimate claim of each man to the expression of his own talents and his own personality—so long as his expression of talents and personality does not infringe unduly upon the rights and contentment of other people. "To each his own" means that every man has the right to seek the fulfillment of his own peculiar nature, to develop to the full the abilities which God has given him, within the bounds of charity and duty. Every man has the natural right to his own abilities and to what he has inherited from his forefathers. In the just state, the energetic man is protected in his right to the fruits of his endeavors; the contemplative man, in his right to study and leisure; the propertied man, in his rights of inheritance and bequest; the poor man, in his rights to decent treatment and peaceful existence; the religious man, in his right to worship; the craftsman, in his right to work. The just state, in short, will endeavor to ensure that no one shall take from another man what properly belongs to his personality, his station in life, and his material interests. The courts are arbiters when these claims seem to conflict. Further, no man shall be above the law; whatever a man's family, fame, wealth, or influence, he shall be expected to abide by the general rules of justice, as expressed in courts of law. The founders of the Republic were resolved that political and legal privilege—that is, exemption of certain powerful persons from the jurisdiction of many of the laws of the land, which then was practiced in nearly all the states of Europe—should not be endured in the United States of America. In America, justice should deal impartially with all claims; justice should be no respecter of persons, though justice should be the guardian of personal rights.

AMERICAN CONCEPT OF EQUALITY

These American statesmen, then, were convinced that men differ in character, talents, and needs. The function of justice is to assure to every man the rights which go with his particular character, talents, and needs. All men ought to be equal before the law; but the law is not intended to force upon them an artificial equality of condition. Justice does not exist in order to change men's natures; rather, justice's purpose is to help men fulfill the particular natures to which they were born. The founders of the Republic did not expect or wish that men ever would be equal in strength, cleverness, beauty, energy, wealth, eloquence, wisdom, or virtue. They did not want a society marked by any such dull uniformity of character. Such a society, in any event, would be impossible to create, they knew; and even were it possible, the result would be boredom and discontent for everyone in it. In one thing only ought men to be equal, here on earth: equally subject to the operation of just laws.

Jefferson, it is true, wrote in the Declaration of Independence "that all men are created equal." But the members of the Continental Congress who subscribed to that Declaration, and probably Jefferson himself, understood by this phrase that all men have natural rights to the development of personality and to equal justice under the law. No American leader of that day supposed that the helpless new-born baby is free, in any literal sense; obviously an infant is not born free, literally, but for a long while is in a condition of the most servile dependence. People are born free only in the sense that they are born to the right to seek what suits their nature. Similarly, the leaders of the young Republic were not so impractical as to think that all men are equal in mind or body or character or inheritance or environment; it was even more obvious in the eighteenth century than now that people are created highly unequal in all these respects. What they understood by the word "equal" in their Declaration of Independence is that all men, regardless of worldly station, enjoy a natural right to equal treatment under the law of the land; no man is privileged by nature to be exempt from the operation of justice. Justice, then, meant to the founders of the Republic the impartial administration of law to secure to every man the things that are his own by nature and inheritance. And this understanding of the nature of justice has for the most part endured in American courts and American public opinion down to our day. Justice does not consist in forcing all people into an artificial and monotonous equality of worldly condition, through the power of the state; such a scheme would have seemed to the Republic's founders monstrously unjust. For the essence of justice is to assure by impartial adjudication that a man may keep whatever is rightfully his and pursue whatever his honest talents fit him for.

Order and Classless Society

What was the nature of order, in the eyes of the men who established the American political system? Proper order, they thought, is necessary to any civilized society. And order means that there must be a recognition of different functions and abilities among the members of society. Any society has its leaders. A justly ordered society will obtain good leaders; a badly ordered society will obtain unscrupulous and incompetent leaders. The founders of the American nation were republicans, but they did not believe for a moment that all men can be leaders; in any age, it is the nature of things that the few must lead and the many follow. They endeavored to ensure that the American Republic might choose its leaders wisely; and that those leaders' power might be hedged and bounded by wise constitutions and counter-balancing influences.

These statesmen of the early years of our country never meant to establish a "classless society." The classless society is the dream of Karl Marx and other nineteenth-century socialists. Classes always had existed in all lands, the Republic's founders reasoned, and classes are a social product of man's nature. There were many classes in their own America, and they expected that there always would be: fishermen, farmers, manual laborers, merchants, artisans, bankers, professional people, clergymen, landed proprietors, teachers, servants, soldiers, sailors, clerks, political administrators, shopkeepers, and yet more orders in society—most of them with a useful and inescapable function, and all of them probably destined to endure, as distinct elements in the nation, to the end of time. There was nothing immoral or obsolete about the existence of class, they felt: class was as natural in society as the separate functions of the brain, the heart, and the lungs in the human body.

MEANING OF ARISTOCRACY

So they did not aspire to abolish class. What they disliked was not class, but *caste*: hereditary distinctions and privileges enforced by law. The granting of titles of nobility, accordingly, was forbidden expressly in the Constitution[2]; and this violated no man's inherited rights, for there were virtually no noblemen in America at the time of the Revolution. The founders of the Republic never aimed at the French vision of absolute equality, as preached by theorists like Condorcet. Though they could not abide caste, they heartily approved of "natural aristocracy"—the leadership of men of unusual talents and large resources. Old John Adams, in correspondence with Thomas Jefferson and John Taylor of Caroline, defined an aristocrat as any man who could influence two votes—his own and someone else's. An aristocrat, in other words, is a natural leader, qualified by intelligence, charm, strength, cleverness, industry, wealth, family, education, or some other resource to influence the opinions of his neighbors. Jefferson, in Virginia, as strongly sup-

ported the claims and rights of an aristocracy of nature as did
Burke, in England. The leaders of American thought and politics knew that any society without honorable leaders must be a
disorderly society. What they foresaw for the future of the Republic was not, then, the abolition of class and superior talents,
but the employment of class and superior talents to the benefit
of the commonwealth.

These American statesmen were neither pure aristocrats
nor pure democrats. They distrusted both aristocracy and democracy, as unmodified forms of government. A satisfactorily
orderly society, they argued, must consist of a mixture of aristocracy and democracy, a balancing and checking and harmo-
nizing of the influence of wealth and private ability with the
influence of numbers and popular desire. They wrote into the
federal constitution and the state constitutions safeguards against
both the power of wealth and the power of needy majorities,
against the ambition of gifted men and the appetite of average
men.

They feared the lust for power of the strong man; and they
feared the lust for possessions of the poor man. They knew that
some unusual and some ordinary men, in any age, will abuse
whatever powers they enjoy. So the founders of the Republic de-
vised a system of constitutional laws—which will be more fully described in the chapter which follows—that would protect decent
social order from either the autocrat or the mob, that would balance the interest and authority of one interest or class in state and

nation against other interests and classes, that would provide a democratically based society with a soundly aristocratic leadership.

"Without order, there is no living together in society": so the authors of the American political system had learned from the English political philosophers, and from their own century and a half of experience in the New World. As nations go, the American Republic has been amazingly orderly, with only one civil war in its history, no successful revolt since the Declaration of Independence, and very few violent protests against the conduct of government. Among the great states of the modern world, only Great Britain—if one excludes Ireland and the British Commonwealth and imperial possessions—has so enviable a record. Every man seeks order in his own life; he is miserable if he lacks it. And every nation that lacks order is bitterly unhappy. The American experiment in the keeping of order remains probably America's proudest just claim to high respect among the nations; it matters far more, for civilization and for American happiness, than the "American standard of living" about which we boast so frequently.

SPECIFIC NATURE OF AMERICAN LIBERTIES

Finally, the leaders of the new American Republic knew very well what they meant when they used the word "freedom." They thought it no paradox that true freedom is obedience to the laws of God. Legitimate freedom, they said, is the right of decent men, governed by conscience, to make their own principal choices in life. And by this they meant no vague abstraction called "Liberty" with a capital L. They were not anarchists, and they were not radical Jacobins. They did not convert their old, sensible, long-cherished English and American freedoms into a cloud-veiled goddess, before whom justice and order must yield pride of place. Most of them, having read John Milton, were well aware of those dangerous persons who "license they mean, when they cry liberty."[3] A few of the American patriots, like Samuel Adams most of his career or Patrick Henry early in life, stood for an absolute and all-embracing liberty of every man to do as impulse bade him; but the great majority, led by prudent men like John Adams, Benjamin Franklin, James Madison, Gouverneur Morris, George Wythe, John Rutledge, James Wilson, John Marshall, Alexander Hamilton, and others—men of every party and faction—desired only a disciplined, traditional, moderate, law-respecting freedom.

Freedom, defined in the negative, is security against having things done to you that you do not wish to have done to you. The civil liberties which colonial America had long enjoyed were of this character; and they were derived from old English liberties, developed and secured over seven centuries. By what was called "a salutary neglect," the English government generally had left the colonists to manage their own affairs, in nearly everything, and thus the thirteen American colonies had grown accustomed to freedom in the conduct of their local concerns and their private lives. Only when the ministers of George III began to assert the absolute and abstract right of king and parliament to make laws for the Americans did the desire for American independence begin to make itself felt. The Americans no longer felt secure that things would not be done to them of which they might not approve; in short, they ceased to feel free. And having been long familiar with freedom, they were willing to risk death for the sake of keeping up that intimacy.

The Americans, therefore, in their petitions to the King of England, in their Declaration of Independence, and in their federal Constitution, did not make the extravagant claims to an unlimited and unhistorical liberty which infatuated the French revolutionaries. In the beginning of their struggle against English power, the colonists asked only that they be confirmed as participants in the long-established "rights of Englishmen." In the Declaration of Independence, they drew up a list of very specific rights to freedom which they felt had been violated or endangered by the King's ministers. In the "Bill of Rights," the ten amendments appended to the Constitution in the first years of the Republic, the American people set down a few definite liberties which expressed precisely what they meant by political freedom. They did not mean by freedom "the absolute right to do whatever we please, regardless of our religion, our duties, and our neighbors." They meant, very differently, certain old and valuable securities against having things done to them, by the state or by powerful men, which they would not relish having done to them. Freedom from interference with religious opinion and worship; freedom from arbitrary arrest; freedom from having troops quartered in one's house; freedom from cruel and unusual punishments; freedom from arbitrary censorship of the press and of speech; freedom from taxation without representation—such were some of the very practical and well-known liberties which they desired to secure. They did not ask for liberation from moral obligations, or from paying rents and debts and taxes, or from the jurisdiction of the courts. They did not ask for freedoms that no political power possibly can guarantee, like "freedom from fear" and "freedom from want."[4] They asked only for the possible: the maintenance or restoration of certain traditional rights of Englishmen and Americans. Freedom, they knew, is not a possession which some prince or president can confer upon men as a gift: not true freedom. Real freedom must be created by individuals and communities. All that central political authority can accomplish is to promise not to abridge the freedoms which men have made for themselves, or which they receive as part of their birthright from God.

Unrestrained Liberty

The founders of the Republic put no trust in absolute, unqualified Liberty. Unrestrained Liberty they thought as dangerous as unrestrained Power. Christian liberty and rightful civil freedoms must be balanced and bounded by the safeguards of conscience, custom, good order, and good constitutions. "O Liberty, what crimes are committed in thy name!" Madame Roland—who was one of the Girondist worshippers of Liberty—cried on her way to the guillotine in Paris. The American statesmen were resolved that, if they could prevent it, no crimes would be committed in Liberty's name in the United States. With few exceptions, their resolution has persisted among Americans down to our decade. Most intelligent Americans today agree with Dostoevski's observation that "If one begins with unlimited freedom, he will end with unlimited despotism." The American cause is not the cause of a revolutionary thirst for demolishing all obstacles to anarchic self-gratification. When modern Americans, like eighteenth-century Americans, use the word "freedom," they mean freedom under law, freedom justified by many years of national experience, freedom under God even. "Men of intemperate minds never can be free," Edmund Burke wrote early in the French Revolution. "Their passions forge their fetters." American freedom has been the liberty of temperate policies and temperate intellects.

American Political Equilibrium

Justice, and order, and freedom: the true polity, the really successful commonwealth, emphasizes equally all three of these. Now and then, in the history of the United States, we have erred by neglecting one of these principles, at some particular moment, or by over-emphasizing another, on a different occasion. Yet, taken all in all, the concepts of the founders of the Republic have endured with a strength and consistency most rare in the course of national destinies. Americans do not presume to argue, if they are wise, that their American institutions might be easily adapted to the needs and ways of other nations; nor that their commonwealth has functioned in every respect better than any other national state. Such self-praise is more liable to vex than to convert our neighbors. But when we hear this little failure of justice in Georgia, or that little neglect of freedom in New York, bewailed and denounced out of all proportion by critics of American institutions, at home or abroad, we have the right to appeal to the perspective of history. Historically judged, the American Republic has maintained a balance of justice and order and freedom for well over two centuries which many nations have not been able to maintain as successfully for even a single year in the whole record of their affairs. Nearly all Americans, on nearly all occasions, can rely, if the necessity arises, upon obtaining impartial justice from the courts; upon being wholly secure in their persons and property through the solidity of American order; upon doing any reasonable thing they like without reprimand. The same could not be said for the glory that was Greece or the grandeur that was Rome.

[1] Editor's note: Latin *cuique suum*.
[2] Editor's note: U.S. Constitution, Article 1, Sections 9, 10.
[3] Editor's note: John Milton, *On the Detraction which followed upon my writing certain Treatises* (1645).
[4] Editor's note: Kirk is alluding to Franklin Delanor Roosevelt's speech, "The Four Freedoms," delivered to the Congress, January 6, 1941.

Chapter Six

POLITICAL PRINCIPLE: THE FEDERAL REPUBLIC

SOURCE OF AUTHORITY

"In questions of power," Thomas Jefferson wrote, "let no more be heard of confidence in man, but bind him down from mischief by the chains of the Constitution." The constitutions of the American commonwealth are intended—and have successfully operated—to restrain political power: to prevent any person or clique or party from dominating permanently the government of the country. Sir Henry Maine, the nineteenth-century historian of law, remarked that the American Constitution is the great political achievement of modern times. The American constitutional system reconciles popular government with private and local rights. It has been called "filtered democracy"—that is, the reign of public opinion chastened and limited by enduring laws, political checks and balances, and representative institutions. It combines stability with popular sovereignty.

It is one of the great premises of American political theory that all just authority comes from the people, under God: not from a monarch or a governing class, but from the innumerable individuals who make up the public. The people delegate to government only so much power as they think it prudent for government to exercise; they reserve to themselves all the powers and rights that are not expressly granted to the federal or state or local governments. Government is the creation of the people, not their master. Thus the American political system, first of all, is a system of limited, delegated powers, entrusted to political officers and representatives and leaders for certain well-defined public purposes. Only through the recognition of this theory of popular sovereignty, and only through this explicit delegation of powers, the founders of the American Republic believed, could the American nation keep clear of tyranny or anarchy. The theory and the system have succeeded: America never has endured a dictator or tolerated violent social disorder.

PURE DEMOCRACY

But in asserting that all power comes from the people, the founders of the Republic had no intention of creating a direct or "pure" national democracy. Early American statesmen—and most of their successors—distrusted popular passions and appetites quite as much as they distrusted the ambitions of strong men. They intended to restrain both the mob and the autocrat. They were not under the illusion that most men and women are naturally good or wise; they knew that neither a great popular majority nor a clever and able minority is fit to be trusted with absolute power. They did not believe that the voice of the people is the voice of God.[1] Although government must exercise considerable power in order to administer justice and defend the commonwealth, nevertheless that necessary power remains always potentially dangerous; it must be held in check by sound constitutions and customs, and by a balancing of the various interests and branches of government, every one of which ought to keep a jealous eye upon the others.

MEANING OF FEDERALISM

Therefore the United States is not a centralized democracy. It does not have government from the top downward; on the contrary, it has government from the bottom upward. Strictly speaking, our government is *federal,* a union of states for certain explicit purposes of general benefit. Federation is very different from centralization. The theory of federation is this, that fifty sovereign states have conferred, of their own free will, certain powers upon the federal administration, to promote the interests of the several states and of the people within those several states. The United States are united voluntarily, and are united only for the purposes, and under the conditions, described in the federal Constitution. In the matters which most immediately affect private life, power remains in the possession of the several states; while within those fifty states, the people reserve to themselves control over most walks of life.[2] The state governments, like the federal government, have been hedged and checked by constitutions and public custom.

LIMITED GOVERNMENT

Everywhere in America, individuals and private voluntary associations jealously reserve to themselves the rights of choice and action in those spheres of activity which most nearly affect the private person. The state touches these private concerns only upon sufferance, or not at all. Religious belief and affiliation are matters wholly of private choice; economic activity, by and large, is left to the will of individuals; social relationships are voluntary and private relationships; where one lives, and how, is not determined by political authority. Quite as much as in England, an American's home is his castle. A great many Americans live their lives through without ever conversing with a civil servant, or even saying more than good morning to a policeman. Americans have no official identity card, or internal passports, or system of national registration. Until 1941, America never experienced peacetime conscription into the armed forces. Nowhere in the world is the operation of government less conspicuous than in the United States. If an American citizen desires to abstain altogether from political activity, even to the extent of never voting, no one interferes with him; and for millions of Americans, their only direct contact with government is their annual submission of income-tax reports. Private life looms much larger than public life in the American commonwealth.

Even in those concerns which have been opened to local or state or federal political activity, the theory persists that political authority operates only as a convenience to private citizens. The public schools, for instance, are intended simply to facilitate the education of young people, not to enforce the educational doctrines of central authority: although the states require that children should be schooled in some fashion, parents with the means are free to educate their children privately, or in de-nominational schools, if they prefer such methods to enroll-ment in public schools. The American assumption is that edu-cation is primarily the concern of the family and the individual, not of the political state; and this frame of mind extends to many more activities in which the state acts as servant, rather than as master.

TERRITORIAL DEMOCRACY

So in America the things in which people are most interested generally remain strictly within the jurisdiction of private life. And in matters of public concern, it is the American habit to keep authority as close to home as possible. The lesser courts, the po-lice, the maintenance of roads and sanitation, the raising of prop-erty-taxes, the control of public schools, and many other essential functions still are carried on, for the most part, by the agencies of local community: the township, the village, the city, the county. American political parties, in essence, are loose local associations: the state and national party organizations are the reflections of local opinion in caucus and town meeting. This state of affairs is what Orestes Brownson, some 150 years ago, called "territorial democracy": popular local control over local affairs, accompanied by strict checks upon state and federal political power. In this sense, the American nation is genuinely democratic, keeping power in the hands of the people.

STATE GOVERNMENTS

What the local community cannot do in the public interest, the state governments generally undertake; only a few matters of national importance are left to the jurisdiction of federal authority. In the courts, the great majority of civil and criminal cases are reserved to the state judges; education, health, and public charity are almost exclusively the concern of state governments, when they are locally administered[3]; road-building and utility-regulation, for the most part, are state functions; the states even have their own military organizations. Though every state is required to give full faith and credit to the acts of all the other states, still they may make what laws and experiments they please, so long as they do not contravene the few and specific limitations written into the federal Constitution. The American states, in short, are very like the Swiss cantons, autonomous for many purposes, and proud of their distinct identity. Many Americans continue to think of themselves as Virginians or Californians or Massachusetts men first, and citizens of the United States second. The belief in states' rights, the view of government which is called "particularism" or "Regionalism," remains strong throughout the country.

Every state has its written constitution, usually more detailed than the federal Constitution, and intended—like the federal Constitution—to put strict limits to the exercise of political power. The state legislatures can draw up public acts only within the scope allowed by the state constitutions, as interpreted by the state supreme courts. Within each of the states, a balance is maintained among the executive, the legislative, and the judicial branches of government. The powers of state governors are limited to the administration of the laws and the vetoing—under certain conditions, differing from one state to another—of bills passed by the legislature; the state judiciary generally maintain their independence of both governor and legislature. As for the fifty legislatures, meeting annually or semi-annually, they too are subject to the American principle of limited and balanced powers: with only one exception—Nebraska, which has a one-chamber legislature—the state legislatures consist of an upper chamber, the senate, and a lower, the house of representatives or assembly. Generally speaking, the state houses of representatives tend to represent population, while the senates tend to represent area, rural constituencies usually predominating in the senates. To the enactment of most legislation, therefore, the consent of house of representatives, senate, and governor is necessary; while the state courts keep watch upon the constitutionality of legislation. The American public has a healthy prejudice against hasty, partial, and arbitrary law-making. In a number of states, the devices of popular initiative, referendum, and recall of public officers lie in reserve as further checks upon men in power.

REPRESENTATIVES

Anyone who wishes to understand American political theory and practice cannot do better than to sit in the gallery of a state senate or house of representatives. From such an observation-post, the meaning of the phrase "filtered democracy" soon becomes clear. Like the members of the national Congress, the members of the state legislatures are not delegates from their constituencies, but genuine *representatives*: that is, they sit in the legislature as men and women of independent judgment, in the tradition of English and American parliamentary usage. They are sent to the legislature not simply to be the mouth-pieces of the voters from their respective districts, but rather to deliberate freely on the innumerable questions of the session; and, by and large, they tend to vote as they please and as they think best. Thomas Jefferson said that although most men are not competent to judge intelligently concerning particular political questions of the hour, nevertheless most men are quite competent to choose representatives qualified to determine such questions; and this remains the theory of American legislative bodies. The state legislatures, like the Congress, represent the popular will, but they endeavor to express that will prudently and conscientiously, and in obedience to the state constitutions. They constitute one of the chief filters of public opinion. On this burning question or that, the better judgment of state legislators may give way before popular agitation or the influence of a powerful lobby; yet throughout their history the state legislative bodies have succeeded, by and large, in reconciling popular demands with prudence and long views. Whatever the deficiencies of particular members of state legislatures, free government in America could not function properly without these representative institutions.

FEDERAL GOVERNMENT

The American federal government is an American state government writ large. The American President is a greater governor; the Congress, a more numerous legislature; the Supreme Court of the United States, a tribunal with the same traditions and procedures as the state supreme courts. For the American states—thirteen of them, at least—are older than the federal government, and served as models for the federal organization. The federal administration is a common government, but not a supreme government: for in many things, the federal government has no authority, those matters being reserved to the states or the people of the states.

The first, second, and third articles of the federal Constitution define, respectively, the rights and duties of the legislative, executive, and judicial powers of the federal government. The legislative power, the Congress of the United States, is composed of two houses, the Senate and the House of Representatives:

the first consists of two senators from each state in the Union, the second of representatives apportioned to each state on the basis of population. Thus the sovereignty of the several states is recognized in the Constitution's first article, for each state has the right to two senators, regardless of population: in the Senate, empty Nevada is as important as crowded New York City. In this, as in many other matters, the United States is not a "pure" democracy; what the framers of the Constitution intended and achieved was not unchecked popular rule, but a judicious balancing and checking of the different interests and states in the Union.

Legislative Power

Until the Seventeenth Amendment was adopted, in 1913, indeed, United States senators were not chosen by popular vote at all, but by the legislatures of the states. The Senate is intended to serve as a kind of aristocracy in the federal government. The terms of senators are for six years; the Senate alone can try impeachments of federal officers; and the Senate alone confirms treaties negotiated by the President, and diplomatic appointments made by him. The United States Senate is the most powerful representative body in the world today.

The federal House of Representatives, a much larger body than the Senate, was intended to serve as the popular branch of the federal legislative power, more directly responsive to public opinion; and its members hold office for two years. The House of Representatives alone can originate bills for raising revenue—a prerogative copied from the colonial assemblies and the English parliament.

In Section Eight of the first article of the Constitution, the powers of Congress are stated explicitly; and, except for such extensions of power as have been granted by later amendments to the Constitution, all powers not specified in this section are reserved to the states or to the people of the states: thus the Congress is not a representative body with powers almost unlimited, like the English Parliament, but rather a limited assembly intended to exercise jurisdiction over certain well-defined matters. The Congress can raise taxes, declare war and peace, maintain armies and navies, borrow money, regulate foreign commerce, coin money, establish post offices and post roads, punish offenses against international law, constitute federal courts inferior to the Supreme Court, grant copyrights and patents, govern federal territories, and do a number of other things intended to promote the general welfare of the United States; but historically the Congress could not intervene in the internal affairs of the several states, nor encroach upon the functions of the executive and judicial branches. Since the foundation of the Republic, the powers exercised by Congress have increased in some significant and unfortunate ways; yet the Congress was intended to be a legislative body of limited authority, not supreme over the nation.

EXECUTIVE POWER

As for the President of the United States, the executive power of the federal system, he now is the most powerful man in the world; and yet his authority is even more severely hedged than is that of Congress. No American President ever has been a real dictator, even in time of war, and if the Constitution continues to function, no President ever will be absolute. Lincoln and Wilson and Franklin Roosevelt were three Presidents whose war-time responsibilities gave them an authority greater than that contemplated by the framers of the Constitution; yet even their emergency-powers could not have been exercised without the concurrence of the Congress, the federal courts, and the majority of the states. The American President may seem to people abroad to be almost a monarch; but at home he remains only the chief magistrate, more limited in his authority than are many European prime ministers.

Very often the political party to which the President happens to belong may be the minority party in both Senate and House of Representatives, since—unlike the prime ministers and premiers of European parliamentary systems—the American President is not a member of the federal legislative branch and is not chosen from Congress. In theory, the President is chosen, every four years, by a body of special "Electors," the Electoral College, who in their turn have been chosen by the people of the several states; but in actuality the Electoral College never has functioned as the framers of the Constitution intended, and the President really is chosen directly by the people of the several states, from among the two or three candidates for the presidency nominated by the chief American political parties.

The President is commander-in-chief of the American army and navy, general supervisor of the federal administration in civil matters, and head of the diplomatic service; he has large powers of pardon and reprieve, and may convene Congress in extraordinary session. As the activities of the federal government have grown, within the United States and abroad, the powers of the President have increased proportionately. Yet it is a remarkable fact that no President ever has endeavored to make himself absolute, and that most Presidents have restrained themselves in the exercise of their legitimate authority. Whenever a President has seemed to seek to increase his power unduly—as, for instance, when Franklin Roosevelt, during his first term in office, sought to obtain control over the Supreme Court through a bill to enlarge its membership—the Congress and public opinion have decided against him, no matter how popular such a President may have been otherwise. Although Congress has the constitutional authority to impeach and remove a President for treason, bribery, and other high crimes and misdemeanors, not a single President has been so removed (though the impeachment process has been initiated several times). When one remembers that the President has no final authority above him—no king, as in the British system, and no permanent president, as in the French system—this record of probity and self-restraint among American Presidents becomes one of the highest achievements of politics in the history of civilization. The American President has powers nearly equivalent to those of the earlier Roman Emperors; but where the Roman system could show only a handful of just and able emperors in the course of centuries, the American system has enjoyed conscientious Presidents without interruption since its inception—and a half-dozen of those Presidents have been men of the highest general abilities.

JUDICIAL POWER

The third great division of the federal government, the judicial power, is dominated by the Supreme Court of the United States, consisting of nine experienced justices who hold office for life, having been appointed by the President. By Constitutional provision, the Supreme Court and the lesser federal courts decide on questions of interpretation of the Constitution; on cases arising under federal law and treaties; on cases affecting ambassadors, ministers, and consuls, and maritime law; on controversies involving the United States and the federal government; on controversies between different states of the Union, between a state and citizens of another state, between citizens of different states, and between American citizens and foreign states or citizens of foreign states. The great bulk of civil and criminal cases in America, however, are in the jurisdiction of the separate state courts.

Early in the history of the Republic, the Supreme Court was secured in its extensive powers and high repute by the strongest of all Chief Justices, John Marshall. Ever since then, with only a handful of exceptions, decisions of the United States Supreme Court have been promptly and voluntarily obeyed as the law of the land. In popular respect, the Supreme Court stands even higher than the Congress and the President. From time to time, the Supreme Court has handed down decisions that were highly unpopular; yet these decisions almost always were accepted and enforced. No other judicial body in all the world is so powerful and so reverenced as is the Supreme Court of the United States. For Americans feel that the Supreme Court, whether or not they agree with its particular decisions at a particular time, in the long run shelters and represents the American principle of liberty under law and the American principle of a government "of laws, not of men."

In general, the Supreme Court has been the stern defender of civil rights, of the rights of property, and of the federal and state constitutions. Throughout most of its history, the majority of justices have recognized the principles of "natural law" as applicable to American society, though there has been some weakening of this belief within the Supreme Court and the other federal courts during the twentieth century. In some periods, the Supreme Court, in questions of constitutional interpretation and the division of powers, has tended to favor the state governments against the federal government; and at other periods, it has leaned toward interpretations which favor the federal government against the state governments. At almost all times the federal courts have acted to protect the individual citizen from encroachments upon his rights by the state or by arbitrary individuals and groups. It is this role of the Supreme Court and the other federal courts as protectors of justice, order, and freedom which has given the federal judiciary such an ascendancy over public opinion.

The federal courts have no armies and navies at their command; their decisions are executed merely by a few federal marshals, appointed by the executive branch. The justices of the Supreme Court are merely nine persons, ordinarily without wealth or even great personal popularity to reinforce their authority. Yet their decisions are obeyed—even by the strongest and most willful of Presidents—quickly and unquestioningly, in nearly every instance. Congress can remove certain classes of legal cases from their jurisdiction, as Congress did during the Civil War; but this Congressional power is very rarely exercised. President Andrew Jackson, angered by Chief Justice Marshall's opinion on one occasion, is said to have declared, "Justice Marshall has made his decision; now let him enforce it." But this attitude of defiance has been almost unique in American history, and President after President has bowed to—and executed—judicial decisions which ran contrary to his plans. There is no better illustration than this of the respect for just authority prevalent in the United States, and of the veneration in which the American Constitution is held by nearly everyone.[4]

Vigor of the American Political System

So the American political system endures to this day, through wars and civil strife, despite immense territorial and population growth in the nation, a system that successfully maintains justice and order and freedom by placing restraints upon power; by keeping sovereignty in the hands of the people, yet preventing mob-rule. Two hundred years is a great while for any political system to thrive unaltered in essence; yet American constitutional structure, despite all the problems of modern society, still seems adequate to the needs of the American nation, and shows few signs of decay. Surely there are very few Americans who advocate any substantial change in the fundamental political institutions of their country—fewer, indeed, than there were a century ago. As Mr. Walter Lippmann suggests in his book *The Public Philosophy*, the present leadership of the United States among the nations thrusts upon the American nation unfamiliar problems of statecraft; but it appears probable that these challenges will be met without serious alteration of the American political foundations. Local rights will continue to be cherished even in an increasingly urbanized and industrialized America; the states will continue to assert their sovereignty; and the three divisions of the federal government will continue to divide federal authority among them.

Political Parties

Now the functioning of this constitutional system has been possible only through the work of free political parties in the United
States. President Washington hoped that "faction," or political
parties, might be unnecessary in the new Republic, but events
proved otherwise. In order to undertake any intelligent political action, in order to chart any course for local or state or
federal government, men and women must associate themselves
in voluntary groups which we call political parties; if party is
lacking, then power slips by default into the hands of private
cliques or demagogues. By and large, the major American parties have been responsible, though loose-knit, organizations.
In the early years of the Republic, the Federalist and Republi-
can-Democratic parties contended against each other; in the
years before the Civil War, the Whig and Democratic parties;
since the Civil War, the Republican and Democratic parties.
This contest, usually, of simply two large parties against each
other has been very like the British experience with the Conservative and Liberal, and the Conservative and Labour, parties; small minority parties, "splinter" parties, do not seem to
fit well into the structure of American or English politics. The
chief European states, on the other hand, have been accustomed to the existence of perhaps a dozen rival parties, form-
ing coalition governments from time to time. If the domination of two great parties possibly has resulted in a less vigorous

expression of minority opinions in the United States, nevertheless the direction of public opinion into one or the other of two enduring groups has helped to give stability to the American political structure.

Two facts ought to be noted concerning these American parties: historically they have not been "ideological," and they have not been tightly organized. When we say they have not been ideological, we mean that they are not fanatical; they do not adhere, ordinarily, to rigid political dogmas at whatever expense to practical consequences in the nation. When we say they have not been tightly organized, we mean that they have little overbearing central direction; the Republican party, or the Democratic party, takes whatever stand on a particular issue that the people "back home," the men and women who attend the village or precinct party caucus, think their party ought to take on that particular issue. The national party program, and the national party candidates, are determined by many thousands of local meetings of interested citizens; and these local meetings are given state-wide expression every two years, in most states, by state party conventions; and nation-wide expression, every four years, by national party conventions.

If, then, it sometimes is said that American parties seem to have no enduring principles, nevertheless we need to remember that neither do they have enduring fanaticisms and errors; and if sometimes it is said that American parties seem to have no permanent leaders, still we need to remember that neither do they have party dictators. Like all other aspects of American political existence, our parties are complex, diverse, cautious, and obedient to the American concept of "territorial democracy." Only once, in all American history, have our parties gone to war; and even then, in the struggle between the states, the alignment of forces was not clearly partisan, for many northern Democrats fought for the Union, and many southern Whigs fought for the Confederacy. Probably a certain vagueness about party doctrines is not a very high price to pay for political peace. Whatever their faults—and most of their old faults, such as the power of party bosses and the spoils-system in appointments to public office, are much diminished nowadays—our political parties have succeeded in enabling representative government to function freely among us. There are only three possibilities beyond moderate political parties: fierce factionalism, dictatorship, and anarchy.

AMERICAN GOVERNMENT AND SOUND SECURITY

The founders of the Republic, and their inheritors, knew what might reasonably be expected of a good society: not Utopia, but a domination of tolerable justice and order and freedom. Commencing from sound philosophical postulates and well-understood historical experience, the leaders of the American nation have succeeded in fulfilling their reasonable hopes. Ours is a truly popular political system, in which the rights of private persons and minorities are protected from temporary majorities by sound constitutions and enduring rules of procedure. As well as any society ever can, probably, we have reconciled the claims of justice and order and freedom. Thinking Americans do not say that the American system of government necessarily is the best system of government for Austria, or Indonesia, or Ethiopia, or the whole world; they say only that it is the best form of government for the United States of America, given our moral and political and economic beliefs and our historical experiences. But they do commend it to other peoples as one successful type of polity, a prudent preference for sound security over dreams of Utopia. The federal Republic of the United States is one of the principal proofs of the American cause.

[1] Editor's note: In Latin, *Vox populi, vox Dei.* Kirk knew that this phrase, coined by Alcuin (c. 735-804), is widely misunderstood and thus widely misused. In his letter to Charlemagne, Alcuin warned, "Do not listen to people who are always saying, 'The voice of the people is the voice of God,' since the riotousness of the crowd always comes close to madness." America's Founders agreed with Alcuin.

[2] Editor's note: This passage needs qualification in light of the last several decades of judicial activism. Landmark Supreme Court cases such as *Griswold v. Connecticut* and *Roe v. Wade*, which nullified state laws, are two obvious examples by which the historic ideal of federalism in America has been eroded.

[3] Editor's note: This assertion is true historically; however, Congress has effectively usurped this authority by controlling the parameters of state welfare law.

[4] Editor's note: The most striking illustration of the public respect accorded the U.S. Supreme Court is the 2000 presidential election. Al Gore received more of the popular vote than did George W. Bush. But the Court's 5 to 4 ruling on the Florida ballot controversy settled the election in Bush's favor. Although there was some initial grumbling among Democrats, it was clear that the vast majority of the American people accepted the legitimacy of the Bush presidency, which in turn was based on the legitimacy of the Supreme Court's decision.

⊰ Chapter Seven ⊱

ECONOMIC PRINCIPLE: THE FREE ECONOMY

REASONS FOR AMERICAN BELIEF IN FREE ENTERPRISE

Political freedom and economic freedom, the great majority of Americans think, are bound together inseparably. Nor can freedom of religious opinion be altogether separated from freedom of economic life. This conviction that a free-market economy is a support of all freedom is one strong motive behind the American championship of what Marxists usually call "capitalism" and what more prudent thinkers usually call our "market economy" or "free enterprise system."

There are other reasons for this American attitude. One of them is the belief that only a society which, by and large, is economically free can be a just society; for the just society is one in which each man may seek the things which belong to his nature. By contrast, a system of economic totalitarianism treats the industrious and the idle, the able and the stupid, as if they were alike—which is contrary to the laws of justice. Another of these reasons is the belief that only a society which, by and large, is economically free can be an orderly society; for the orderly society is one in which every class and interest fulfills the functions for which it is best suited. Without economic freedom a class of economic autocrats could domineer over all other elements in society. Yet one more reason is the belief that the value of a system may be judged by that system's fruits, and the free economies of modern times, particularly in the United States, have been economically fruitful.

"It will take some hammering to drive a coddling socialism into America," George Santayana once wrote. Yes, and the proportion of professed socialists is smaller in the United States, indeed, than it was when Santayana wrote. The great American labor unions never have flirted long with economic collectivism, and the number of economic radicals among educated people is smaller in the United States than in most countries; while the American merchant and industrialist remained undismayed champions of economic competition and free enterprise. Yet it remains possible for a nation to lose economic freedom through a failure to understand the necessary conditions of such freedom, just as it is possible for a people to lose political freedom in a fit of absence of mind. Our first necessity, then, is to apprehend the theories that lie behind the reality of our free-market economy.

DANGER OF EXAGGERATED ECONOMIC SLOGANS

Sometimes, indeed, vociferous American devotees of "American capitalism" and "the American standard of living" do more mischief than benefit to their own cause, generating more heat than light, and substituting facile slogans for first principles. It is presumptuous to urge an American soldier, for instance, to die for his standard of living; and an American soldier would have to be very stupid to do anything of the sort. If by "standard of living" is meant simply the material goods and services that people happen to enjoy, it is folly to die for this; since the only way to enjoy a standard of *living* is to live. And it would be still more foolish to die for someone else's standard of living. To die for religion, justice, order, freedom, honor, or the lives of other people usually is a noble act. But to die for one's own creature-comforts, or for someone else's creature-comforts, always is a very ridiculous act. It is an insult to an American soldier to ask him to die for a new automobile or an apple pie; but it is a compliment to an American soldier to ask him to die for the ashes of his fathers and the temples of his God.

ECONOMIC PRODUCTION A MEANS TO ENDS

So we ought not to exaggerate the importance of our economic arguments or of our American economy. In many ways, the free-market economy of the United States is a good thing in itself; yet it is not the whole of life. No economy, however productive materially, could be a good thing if it were founded upon injustice, disorder, slavery, and dishonor. The slave-labor camps of the Soviet Union were economically efficient, after a fashion—but only because they took no reckoning of human lives or moral principles. Thus our American economy, though good in itself, is important not merely for its own sake: its real importance is the contribution it makes to our justice and order and freedom, our ability to live in dignity as truly human persons. Our "standard of living," though often enjoyable in itself, is not the be-all and end-all of life. Economic production is merely the means to certain ends. One of those ends is the satisfaction of man's material wants. And there are other ends served by this means of economic production: the satisfaction of certain profound desires in human nature, such as the desire for fruitful work and sufficient leisure and hopeful competition, for one; and the maintenance of a decent society, for another.

Now in the economic realm, what is the American cause? It is the defense of an economic system that allows men and women to make their own principal choices in life; which reinforces political liberty; which adequately supplies the necessities of life; which recognizes and guides beneficently the deep-seated human longing for competition and measurable accomplishment. What we call the "free-market economy" does these things.

Marx and "Capitalism"

Karl Marx, the chief exponent of modern socialism, popularized both the term "capitalism" and the term "communism." Marx thought that all of life is merely an exercise in economics:

he would have cast religion aside altogether, and would have made literature and the arts merely the slaves of politico-economic movements, and would have sacrificed freedom, gladly, to his idol of economic equality. His latter-day disciples, the Communists of the Soviet Union and their allies, maintained these radical doctrines in all their rigor. "Communism," in theory, is the ownership of all property, collectively, by "the workers"; and the distribution of all goods and services according to need—so far as possible, on terms of exact equality—regardless of individual differences and private rights. (In practice, modern applied communism has not worked out this way at all; but that is another matter.) Material production is the whole end and aim of a Communist society: material goods are all that make life worth living, in the eyes of the thoroughgoing Communist; and for the thoroughgoing Communist, there can be no life except the fleeting life which we experience here and now, on this earth.

Against this Communist ideal, Marx set an economic society which he called "capitalism": the economic system that prevailed in his own day. Marx hated many things; but most of all he hated capitalism and its works. By "capitalism," he meant an economic system in which the means of production are owned by private persons. Marx believed that such a system defrauded the workers of their just due, caused wars, and led inevitably to social decay. Once capitalism was thoroughly extirpated, Marx argued, all men would be free. To attain this perfect society of communism, Marx predicted, the working classes, the "proletariat," would revolt fiercely against their capitalist masters, seize the means of production, establish a proletarian dictatorship, turn the world upside down, and eventually watch the state wither away until everyone might enjoy the fruits of economic production without masters or duties. And this would be the end of history; thereafter, mankind would live forever in a changeless state of satisfaction.

MEANING OF COMMUNISM

To most Americans, substantially content with their own country's social and economic order, the vision of Marx seems a ludicrous caricature of the modern economy and a hopelessly fantastic grasping after what never can be. Yet Marx's writings succeeded, in combination with other factors, in turning half the world inside out. Uniting with the discontent which always is present in any society, and with disturbances in modern society that accompany the spread of the industrial revolution and the decay of old ways of life, Marxism became a political religion, an ideology, conquering half of Europe and three-fourths of Asia, and influencing opinion nearly everywhere else, quite as speedily as Mohammedanism spread across Asia and Africa twelve centuries ago.

There is not space here to refute the doctrines of Marxism in detail; and, besides, most Marxists are not affected by mere logical argument. "To consider whether Marx was 'right' or 'wrong';

to dredge Volumes I and III of *Das Capital* for inconsistencies or logical flaws, to 'refute' the Marxian system," Professor Alexander Gray writes, "is, in the last resort, sheer waste of time; for when we consort with Marx we are no longer in the world of reason or logic. He saw visions—clear visions of the passing of all things, much more nebulous visions of how all things may be made new. And his visions, or some of them, awoke a responsive chord in the hearts of many men." It is also not of much use to inquire whether Soviet Communism was "true Marxism"; for "true Marxism" never can be attained so long as human beings remain human. Soviet Communism is simply what any society falls into when it makes the terrible experiment of overthrowing established justice and order and freedom in the pursuit of that will-o'-the-wisp called communism.

ADAM SMITH

All we shall try to do in this chapter is to state quite simply the principles which lie behind the free economy that we know in America. These are principles which thinking men and women have understood, in part at least, for a great many centuries. They were expressed afresh, and more systematically than before, near the close of the eighteenth century, most notably by a Scottish professor of moral philosophy, Adam Smith. The teachings of Adam Smith and other British and French political economists were widely read and applied by the American generation that established the Republic. Although some of the doctrines of the eighteenth- and nineteenth-century economists have been modified by subsequent speculation and experience, for the most part the case for a free economy remains as Smith put it. The wealth of nations, Smith wrote, depends upon an economy in which there are free competition, sufficient reward for private industry and private saving, and reliance upon ordinary motives and ordinary virtues. Such a society, such an economy, is guided by an "invisible hand": the natural law of economic existence which rules that every man, though laboring for his own benefit, actually increases the common good through his private labors. It is a powerful case that Smith puts.

DEFINITION OF CAPITAL

We may call this system of free enterprise "capitalism," if we like, though that Marxist word does not really mean very much. "Capital" is simply those goods—tools, machines, buildings, ships, trains, and the like—which are used to produce other goods. Any civilized society, therefore, is "capitalistic," since capital goods always are required to produce consumer goods. A communistic society requires capital quite as much as a "capitalistic" society does. But what Marx meant by "capitalism" is the ownership of capital by private persons. In that sense, America undoubtedly is a capitalistic country; nowhere else in the world, in any age, has the ownership of capital been as widespread as it is today, directly or indirectly, in the United States.

And the defense of this economy is an important part of the American cause.

IDEA OF COMPETITION

At the heart of the theory of the free economy lies the idea of competition. Something in human nature seems to call for the possibility of a real victory in life—and the possibility of a real defeat. Life is enjoyable because hope exists: hope for success of one sort or another. And hope for success cannot exist without a corresponding dread of failure. In a very real sense, life is a battle; we never could be happy were it otherwise. The strong enjoy struggling against obstacles; life without obstacles is boredom, just as life without purposeful work is infinitely dreary. Even were it possible—which it is not—for men and women to spend all their time idly, they would be terribly bored by such an existence. To be rich without duties or challenges—to be the "idle rich" long denounced by the radical agitator—is to be unhappy all one's life. Human beings are content only when they are struggling against obstacles: and the form which that struggle ordinarily takes we call competition.

Most of us enjoy competing against our neighbors, in one fashion or another; and, naturally, the instinct for competition is strongest in the more energetic and able men and women. Through competition, talents are developed and utilized which otherwise would be neglected; even the losers profit from the existence of competition, because the abilities and the goods produced by the able in the competitive struggle benefit everyone in society. Now competition takes various forms; and if it is competition without any moral checks, it can be vicious. Competition of any sort ought to be governed by conscience and the rules of morality. Yet, by and large, competition is the means through which most improvement of society is accomplished: intellectual competition, and military competition, and economic competition. And economic competition, when restrained by moral principles, almost always does good to everyone in society. As Samuel Johnson said once, "A man is seldom more innocently occupied than when he is engaged in making money." This economic competition is essential to a free economy.

Motives to Integrity

"Ordinary integrity," Edmund Burke wrote, "must be secured by the ordinary motives to integrity." Men and women are industrious, thrifty, honest, and ingenious in economic life only when they expect to gain certain rewards for being industrious, thrifty, honest, and ingenious. Some few human beings, in any age, work simply out of altruism, desire to benefit their fellows; but the vast majority work principally out of self-interest, to benefit themselves and their families. There is nothing wrong with this state of affairs; it is merely a condition of ordinary human nature. Competition puts a premium on industry, thrift, honesty, and ingeniousness. The slothful, the spendthrift, the known cheats, and the stupid fall behind in the economic contest of free enterprise. Yet even these latter share to some extent in the benefits of competition, since the abilities and the goods developed by their more successful neighbors are distributed to the whole of society. The more industry, thrift, honesty, and ingeniousness the world can encourage, the better off the whole world is. By following their own self-interest, able men and women serve the public interest. And the habits and skills which intelligent competition stimulates tend to improve, by example, even the less able members of society, while the rewards of successful competition, in terms of prestige and material gain, serve as the ordinary motives to ordinary integrity. Industry, thrift, honesty, and ingeniousness deserve concrete rewards. A competitive economy provides those rewards.

COMPULSION AS A SUBSTITUTE

If a society is deprived of competition, it is forced to rely either upon altruism (the unselfish efforts of men and women who work without reward) or upon compulsion (force employed to make people work without reward). Now the number of utterly unselfish men and women always is very small—insufficient to provide for the wants of the mass of society. And the use of compulsion to enforce work and a semblance of industry, thrift, honesty, and ingeniousness is slavery—incompatible with a free society and the concept of the dignity of man. Therefore a society without economic competition either falls into a dismal decay, because there are not enough unselfish people to do the world's work, or else it falls into slavery, the degradation of human nature and civilization. It has been said that there are two ways to persuade a donkey to carry his load: to show him a carrot, or to show him a stick. Mankind carries the load of the world's work for one of two reasons: either because of the incentive of ordinary rewards for ordinary integrity, the carrot; or else because of the hard punishment of failure, the stick. It is much more pleasant to live in a society with the promise of carrots than in a society with the threat of sticks. When the Communists swept away economic competition and abolished all the old motives to ordinary integrity, they found themselves compelled to resort to severe punishments in order to get work done at all. The slave-labor camps, the industrial spies and informers, the rigid production-quotas for factories and individuals, the enslavement of whole nations, are the manifest consequences of abolishing competition.

And free labor generally is much more effectual than servile labor. When men and women work for their own improvement, they work with the best that is in them; but when they work only because of fear of the stick, they do as little as possible. Economically and morally, a competitive system is nothing to be ashamed of. On the contrary, it provides for human wants and respects human freedom far better than can any vague scheme of reliance solely upon altruism, or any system of forced labor. In essence, it is not competition which is ruthless; rather, it is the lack of competition that makes a society ruthless; because in a competitive economy people work voluntarily for decent rewards, while in a non-competitive economy a few harsh masters employ the stick to get the work done.

CHARITY AND COMPETITION

A competitive society in which sound moral principles prevail is not a selfish or ruthless society. Through charity, such a society provides for the needs of those who, because of one handicap or another, cannot provide for themselves in the economic contest. The successful, in such a society, are taught by moral precepts that it is their moral duty to give voluntarily to their neighbors who stand in need of aid. Competition does not rule out love and compassion. In a genuinely competitive society, most such acts of charity are ideally private and local, the work of individuals and voluntary organizations, though in emergencies and in cases beyond the scope of private action the government takes a hand. Enlightened competition does not mean "dog eat dog." Successful competition makes possible successful charity; for the increased productivity of a competitive free economy gives society the surplus of goods and services with which to relieve the poor, the infirm, the disabled, the old, and the young.

A free economy is one in which men and women can make their own choices. They can choose the kind of work they want to do, and where they want to do it. They can buy what they choose, and abstain from what they choose. They can work when they like, within limits, and rest when they like. They can change occupations and employers and their material circumstances as much as they like. These are great benefits; they help satisfy the fundamental human longing for self-reliance. They make men and women free.

SERVILE ECONOMY

But an economy without competition is a system in which men and women are allowed almost no free choices. It is a regimented, a servile, economy. In such a system, everything must be totally planned. A small body of persons, who are the real masters of society under such circumstances—called commissars, or planners, or what you will—must determine what is to be produced, and who is to receive it, and who shall do what work, and what people shall be paid, and where and how long they shall work, and how they shall be punished if they do not work. Even questions of taste and style must be fixed by a bureau under such a regime. Such a system keeps men and women in perpetual childhood, their wants provided for by central authority, and their choices, in proportion, made for them by central authority. Human life under such conditions discourages the full development of mind and character. A great critic of literature, George Saintsbury, expressed with loathing the general curse of such a society: "Put away all thought of the crime and agony which would have to be gone through in order to bring about the Socialist Utopia; get it somehow brought about by fairy agency; could there, even then, be anything more loathsome than one wide waste of proletariat-Coquecigrue comfort; everybody as good as the President; everybody as 'well educated' as everybody else; everybody stationed, rationed, regulated by some kind of abstract 'State'—as equal, and really as free, as pigs in a sty, and not much better deserving the name of man, or the manly chances of position, possession, genius, ancestry, and all that differentiates us from the brutes?"

The collectivistic economy necessarily abolishes every sort of freedom, for men and women must eat; and if some central authority is able to tell them whether or not they shall eat, and how much, and under what circumstances, they are the slaves of that central authority, even though that totalitarian economic system may call itself "democratic." Compulsory labor under the direction of powerful administrators is the most conspicuous feature of any functioning regimented economy. The worker who fails to obey, or to produce a quota, is denounced as a "saboteur," and every stimulus to private initiative and ingenuity is discouraged. In exchange for a fancied economic security—in exchange for a promise from the state to supply all the necessities of life—half the world gave up its economic freedom. But this is a devil's bargain, for with economic freedom, political freedom and private rights also vanish. And the totalitarian state does not fulfill its part of the bargain, since once the old motives to industry and thrift and honesty and ingenuity have been swept away, the driving force behind a country's system of economic production is terribly weakened; production declines and invention languishes; even the ferocious powers of compulsion exercised by the totalitarian state seldom compensate for the decline of private integrity and competition. In the so-called global economy of our times, it really is not possible to buy economic security at the price of liberty. It is possible only to surrender freedom in exchange for total planning—which relieves most people of the necessity for making their own choices in life, but also relieves them of their prosperity and their birthright as human beings.

SOCIAL JUSTICE, TRUE AND FALSE

So the free economy, characterized by liberty of choice, private ownership of capital, and competition, is a bulwark of all freedom. It also is a bulwark of justice. Justice, we ought not to forget, means "to each his own"—to each man the things that suit his own nature. Zealots for economic collectivism talk a great deal about "social justice"—by which they mean that all people ought to have an equal share in the world's goods. Closely examined, however, their theories can produce only social injustice; for once applied, those theories deprive men and women of the rewards that belong to their nature. Even Karl Marx knew that Communism must treat unfairly—in any established meaning of the word "fairness"— the abler and more talented people. "In order to establish equality," Marx wrote in *Das Kapital,* "we must first establish inequality." By this he meant that the Communistic state will take away

from the strong, the clever, the thrifty, the ingenious, the de-
pendable—from all the people who have unusual abilities and
savings—and would give their property and the product of their
energies to the weak, the dull, the improvident, the routine-
minded, the slack. For complete equality of condition in this
world can be established only if a society is willing to penalize
the better natures in order to benefit the less gifted natures. If
we believe in the idea of justice that lies at the root of classical
and Christian thought, such an undertaking would be not justice, but gross injustice; it would deny to most of the better
men and women the things that belong to their nature—the
rewards of private integrity.

Pure Equality Impossible

Nor is such a complete equality possible in any society. It has
not come to pass in any of the Communistic states, for there
the commissars and party leaders enjoy power and material rewards immensely greater than the average. Leadership, whether
it is good or bad leadership, always will exact rewards. It is possible, through revolution or unjust laws, to abolish the prop-
erty-rights and the incomes of the possessors of capital and the
leaders of society. But it is not possible to abolish leadership
and the necessary rewards of leadership. All that Communist
revolutions accomplished, in reality, was to supplant the old
leadership by a host of squalid oligarchs spewed up by the violence of the revolution; and it turned out that the new political

and economic masters were far harder and less charitable than
the old.

TOTALIST ECONOMY AND DISORDER

A regimented economy is unjust, then, and also it is disorderly.
For order means that a society recognizes its natural leaders, in
their rightful functions: its principled statesmen, its holy clergy,
its learned scholars, its energetic men of business, its skilled
craftsmen; it gives all these, and all other orders in society, their
due. But the collectivistic economy abolishes all these distinctions and functions, substituting for the healthy variety of a free
economy a new elite of bureaucrats and party agents who usurp
the functions and the rewards of all those beneficial orders.
There remain in the totalitarian economy only two classes: the
arrogant new elite of managers and planners, and the faceless
crowd of the "proletariat," subservient to the demands of the
total state. Through the employment of force and surveillance,
such a collectivistic state may keep the peace; but it is hopelessly disordered in the sense that it has repudiated the principles of free choice and natural leadership.

It is not the American mission to compel or persuade all the
world to copy "American capitalism." If the American people
believe in free choice at home, they must support the principle of
free choice among nations. America has no moral imperative, for
instance, to abolish the communal system of land-cultivation prevalent in Java, or to make the Swiss give up their system of state-

owned railways. Every nation must choose its own institutions. But Americans do have the right, and the duty, to defend their own free economy, with all its benefits, against collectivistic attack or subversion: to defend their economy in the interest of freedom and justice and order and prosperity. And Americans do have the right to assist other countries in which a free economy is menaced by the designs of the economic collectivists; for even the vigorous American economy would have difficulty surviving in a world dominated by totalitarian states. Whatever its shortcomings, the American system of free enterprise has given our nation a prosperity very rare in any age; and it is infinitely freer and juster and more orderly than any collectivistic scheme of total regulation.

⁓ Chapter Eight ⁓

ECONOMIC PRINCIPLE:
AMERICAN ECONOMIC ACCOMPLISHMENT

AMERICAN STANDARD OF LIVING

The greatness and contentment of a nation are not measured merely by that nation's wealth. Compared with any modern state, Athens in the fifth century before Christ was extremely poor; but the world has not seen since such intellectual brilliance as then resided in Athens. One of the most remote and thinly populated of modern countries, Iceland, appears to be at once among the most nearly contented and the most highly cultured of nations; while some of the states with the larger national incomes also have the higher rates of suicide and crime. So although American prosperity is something for which Americans ought to be thankful, nevertheless they ought not to rest their whole case, when they defend the American cause, upon the evidences of American wealth. Braggart nations, like braggart men, generally are disliked; and smugness is a dangerous mood for any country, no matter how great its natural resources may be.

Yet, this said, the United States undeniably is a great economic success. Part of this success results from our natural resources; part from our size as a nation, which gives us one of the largest free-trade areas in the world; and part—probably the most important part—from the economic and political and moral principles by which we govern ourselves.

Concentration of Wealth

America's wealth is widely distributed. The nation's citizens have the power to enjoy standards of diet, housing, and physical comfort previously unknown to humankind. During the Great Depression, certain radical agitators invented the slogan that "5 percent of the people own 95 percent of the wealth in the United States." This slogan was, and is, a baseless fabrication. Never before, in any civilized society, has there been a greater distribution of wealth than there is now in America. According to some economists, indeed, the trouble may be that we do not reward well enough the "upper classes," the more energetic and thrifty people among us.

The real income of Americans continues to rise steadily, and is reflected in private savings and in our "people's capitalism," through which more and more Americans are coming to own a share in American industry. Most of our "capitalists" are people of moderate means, who own stocks or bonds or insurance policies invested in large commercial and industrial corporations; millions of our private investors are men and women who work with their hands. American labor unions, indeed, now are "capitalists" in their own right, since the gigantic pension funds and reserves of the unions usually are invested in the stocks and bonds of "private" corporations. One index of our general prosperity and stability, extending to every order in American society, is the steady increase in the number of houses privately owned by their occupants; among the great states, America stands first in the world in family ownership of homes. Although local, state, and federal governments have undertaken large-scale projects of slum-clearance and low-rent public housing, these developments are much more modest, in proportion to the total population, than they are in much of Europe; and the reason for this is that most American families are able, and willing, to pay for their own houses.

AMERICAN MATERIAL ACHIEVEMENTS

In education—at the primary, secondary, and advanced level—Americans spend more per capita than any other people; we have far more students, per head of population, enrolled in institutions of higher learning than has any other country. In medical treatment and hospitalization, we are better off than any other nation; voluntary private health-insurance organizations provide the American alternative to socialized medicine. We have reduced the worries of old age by elaborate systems of pensions and insurance, both private and public. And our economy seems remarkably stable, as national economies go; we have had no stock-market "crash" since 1929, and our periods of recession or temporary unemployment seem to be increasingly brief and moderate. No one need starve in America. We take this fact so much for granted that we tend to forget what a remarkable fact it is. Until well into the nineteenth century, throughout the world, on the contrary, starvation was taken for granted; it was thought inevitable that, from time to time, thousands or even millions of men and women and children must starve in times of famine or industrial disorder. In much of the developing world, occasional starvation still is taken for granted.

TECHNOLOGY AND FREEDOM

Our American prosperity is not simply an accident. Our technology, our industrial ingenuity, has much to do with our economic success, of course; but that technology, in considerable part, is itself the product of a free economy. For a free economy offers great material rewards to invention, efficiency, and shrewd management. Competition tends to eliminate the inefficient and obsolete, and to put a premium upon new methods and discoveries. An industrialist or a merchant is responsible for his own blunders, and is entitled to the profits of his ability, under a system of free enterprise. Ideally, business is generally left to businessmen, as it ought to be, except for a minimum of regulation in the interest of fair play; and technology is left to the technicians and scientists. A man works best when he works freely, for his own advantage. His inventions and increases of capital may be initially for his own benefit, but in the long run they benefit all society.

FREE ENTERPRISE AND LEISURE

Marx was wrong: free enterprise does not lead to servitude and poverty for the masses. By liberating energies, a free economy encourages people to do their best. It is free enterprise, indeed, that has abolished slavery in the Western world. Slavery exists either when many people will not work hard enough or long enough except under compulsion, or when the only way to provide that leisure essential to society seems to be to make some people work hard and long in order that a minority may have leisure for thought and leadership. The classical world saw no alternative to slavery; the Old South saw no alternative to slavery. But whatever the age of competition and free enterprise has done or failed to do, certainly it has emancipated the mass of men and women from involuntary labor. Until the triumph of modern industry—which went hand in hand with the triumph of a free economy—it was possible to obtain leisure only by living upon the labor of others, or by living in poverty, foregoing creature comforts in the interest of the contemplative life. But today, and especially in America, it is possible for everyone to have relatively abundant leisure: this is the fruit of industrial efficiency and a free economy.

Nowadays most Americans work only forty hours a week—a vast improvement over the conditions of a century past. There is talk even of a four-day week. For the mass of people, such a quantity of free time is a novelty, so that some spend their free hours only in idleness, which is boring. We have increased the leisure of people who work with their hands, indeed, more greatly than we have increased the leisure of people who work with their minds. Every element in our society has shared in the benefits of our prosperity. Even our farmers, despite frequent complaints, are better off economically than they used to be, most of them; it is only relatively that they have not kept up, in recent years, with the prosperity of their city cousins. Farm income, in short, has increased, but has not increased so much as has the income of people in manufacturing and the service industries; yet the farmer, in terms of work and comfort, now has a much easier life than had his father or grandfather.

PROSPERITY NO GUARANTEE OF HAPPINESS

Economic prosperity cannot guarantee human happiness. Happiness, for that matter, is very difficult to define. Who is happier, J. F. Stephen asks in his book *Liberty, Equality, Fraternity*: "a very stupid prosperous farmer who dies of old age after a life of perfect health, or an accomplished delicate woman of passionate sensibility and brilliant genius, who dies worn out before her youth is passed, after an alternation of rapturous happiness with agonies of distress?" And, Stephen says, this is like "asking the distance from one o'clock to London Bridge";

one man's happiness is another man's pain. Mankind never is perfectly content either with work or with leisure; the rich are not free from care, and prosperous nations still have their problems. So Americans are imprudent if they argue that American prosperity demonstrates the superiority of all American institutions. It is entirely possible for a Portuguese peasant or an Austrian monk to be happier than an American businessman, though it is not possible for him to be richer. When the American talks of freedom to the people of India, he tends to fall into the error of identifying freedom with material prosperity. But for the Indian who knows his native traditions, "freedom" means the absence of worldly desire, and thus the American merely puzzles him; besides, it is improbable that India ever can be one-third so prosperous as the United States, so boasts of American wealth may merely excite envy. We ought not to make too much of the economic argument when we are defending the American cause.

So far as material achievement can satisfy human longings, nevertheless, we Americans have gone further than have any other people; and we have diffused our prosperity more widely throughout our nation. To leaf through the annual *Statistical Abstract of the United States* is to obtain overwhelming proof of our economy's success. And anyone who has traveled a little in America sees the evidences of a tremendous material accomplishment on every hand—a prosperity expressed in better houses, better food, new automobiles, great schools and public buildings, splendid highways, a multitude of popular luxuries. In the face of all this evidence, how can doctrinaire statists continue to argue that America is a land of capitalistic oppression and failure?

AMERICAN ECONOMY CONTRASTED WITH TOTALIST ECONOMY

American society is imperfect; but all human societies are imperfect in some degree. The American economy has its faults; but they are faults that may be modified. A free economy, because of its opportunities for choice and competition, has always within it the possibilities of improvement; it does not repress the reformer. But a totalitarian economy, hostile to any sort of criticism, founded on envy and terror, cannot amend its ways without ceasing to be; it leaves no room for prudent reformation. When something in a free economy goes wrong, there is temporary trouble, but the variety of talents and the elasticity of the economic structure make mending fairly easy. When, however, something in a totalitarian economy goes wrong, there is general and serious suffering, because the master-plan of the regimented economy is inelastic and arbitrary. The free economy, in such conditions, penalizes only a few by loss of profit, or resort to bankruptcy. But when the totalitarian economy is brought to account for its mistakes, it seeks scapegoats; and the concentration camp substitutes for the bankruptcy-court.

AMERICAN ECONOMIC PROBLEMS

It will not do for us to be complacent about our American economy. We have many grave problems. We need to humanize mass-production, and to restore craftsmanship and personal accomplishment to work, and to teach ourselves how to make our leisure something better than boredom. We need to infuse into modern life a sense of community and purpose and hope and deep-rooted security. We need more genuinely educated businessmen and more genuinely responsible labor-union leaders. We need decentralization of industry and more penetrating regard for the claims of rural life.

But none of these problems can be solved by economic collectivism. Communism, the sham of "total economic planning," is death to prosperity, as it is fatal to freedom. It abolishes the ordinary motives to ordinary integrity; for enlightened self-interest, it substitutes a new and more thorough slavery. It rewards intrigue and betrayal; it punishes honesty and diligence and charity. In the name of making all men equal, it makes all men servile. Its claims run counter to the deepest instincts of human nature. What is unnatural never can make men happy. Communism abolishes the opportunities for personal advancement and enduring accomplishment which our economic system has made available to all people willing to work. In upholding a free economy, Americans are upholding the material fabric of an elevated civilization.

❧ Chapter Nine ❧

ANTI-AMERICAN CLAIMS

In every age there is much human discontent, and in nearly every age there arises some revolutionary movement which takes advantage of that discontent.

DISCONTENT PRODUCED BY CHANGE, CONFUSION

We would be smug and silly to deny that there are reasons for discontent with modern life. It is not ordinarily poverty that creates discontent, for the great majority of people usually have been poor and yet reasonably contented with their lot. It is not lack of wealth that necessarily produces modern discontent and opens the gates to revolutionary movements. What really creates discontent in the modern age, as in all ages, is confusion and uncertainty. People turn to radical doctrines not necessarily when they are poor, but when they are emotionally and intellectually distraught. When faith in their world is shaken; when old rulers and old forms of government disappear; when profound economic changes alter their modes of livelihood; when the expectation of

private and public change becomes greater than the expectation of private and public continuity; when even the family seems
imperiled; when people can no longer live as their ancestors
lived before them, but wander bewildered in new ways—then
the radical agitator, of one persuasion or another, has a fertile
field to cultivate. Men do not often rebel against mere privation, but they frequently revolt against the confusion of their
society. And usually their rebellion only makes that confusion
worse confounded.

Thus it is the giddy pace of change in the modern world that
has generated our modern discontents. So far as technology is
concerned, there has been more change in the past two centuries
than in the whole preceding three thousand years; and in some
lands, this change of technology, which we usually call the "industrial revolution," has been compressed into a single generation of
the twentieth century. Roughly parallel with these revolutionary
technological changes in civilization have come social and intellectual changes equally catastrophic, such as the decay of established religious and moral beliefs, the malfunctioning of old political institutions, and an immense increase in population over
much of the world. It is no wonder that men and women have
found it difficult to adjust themselves to this giddy change. But to
turn the world upside down in resentment at the world's confusion is no remedy.

We can discern in history other such ages of confusion produced by rapid change, such as the fifth century before Christ in

Greece, and the first century before Christ in Rome. In those times, too, confusion led to revolution, war, and tyranny. In the twentieth century, revolutions were produced by this confused protest at the rapidity of change. People embrace fantastic proposals when they are bewildered and insecure. The Nazis came to power in Germany, the most prosperous and energetic and best-schooled of European nations, upon the wave of this confused discontent. The Communists of Russia took advantage of the Russian defeat in the First World War to impose themselves upon that immense country. The Communists in China rose upon the ruin of the ancient Chinese civilization. The Communists of central Europe triumphed only because—aside from the support of Russian armies—Europe was utterly bewildered in the aftermath of the Second World War. When people have lost their accustomed beliefs and their established ways of life—whether they are rich or poor—they tend to seek some political religion, some fanaticism which promises them peace of body and mind. Knowing this ancient weakness in human nature, revolutionaries of the twentieth century have been able to make themselves attractive to many in the developing world. They have flourished by the indecision and groping discontent of the majority of people.

COMMUNISM AND IDEOLOGY

A revolutionary movement, such as communism or Nazism, is not truly a reasoned social philosophy, but instead what is properly called an "ideology": a fanatic political creed that promises to its disciples what no simple political or economic alteration really can accomplish. It is, as Burke said of Jacobinism in the French Revolution, "an armed doctrine." It holds forth to the confused and discontented the Utopia of a classless society, in which all material wants will be supplied without personal responsibility, and in which change will have been abolished. What it promises is a caricature of the Christian vision of Heaven. It is Heaven upon earth, but with God eliminated. Philosophically and historically speaking, the ideological Utopian is mad. But that fact does not diminish his appeal to a great many people. In revolutionary times, as Alexis de Tocqueville writes, madness may be an advantage, leading to temporary success. Utopian ideologues promise what neither they nor anyone else can perform: that is, they promise to make human nature and society perfect by changing laws and social institutions. Their Utopia must always remain Nowhere-Land. Some apologists for communism, embarrassed by the Russian example, argued that Russian communism is not "true" communism. This apology is correct in one sense only: that "true" communism is impossible to establish in Russia or anywhere else. For "true" communism is hopelessly impractical, running contrary to everything we know about human nature and society.

PURE COMMUNISM IMPOSSIBLE

Communism is, and has always been, an illusion: in its "true" or "pure" form, it never can be established among men—nor can any abstract revolutionary movement. Yet it is entirely possible, as the modern world knows to its cost, for persons calling themselves Communists to seize power, establish "Soviet Republics," and destroy order and justice and freedom and the finest works of civilization. What these triumphant revolutionaries bring to a nation is not the promised Heaven upon earth—which is impossible—but a very real Hell upon earth. They can erect, and perhaps maintain indefinitely, a tyrannical regime which they describe as "Socialist," and which, they declare, is progressing toward, say, "communism." This "progress" usually consists of the extirpation of all opposition and the complete physical and intellectual subjugation of the people upon whom they have imposed their iron regime. Pure communism, pure radical utopianism of any kind, is a delusion; but the power they wield is often a grim reality.

REVOLUTIONARIES NOT REASONABLE MEN

So it is important to understand what manner of men most revolutionaries are, and what doctrines they profess, and what arguments they employ to make converts, and particularly what accusations they make against the United States. As Professor Gerhart Niemeyer writes in his book *An Inquiry into Soviet*

Mentality, these Communist doctrines and arguments and accusations and tactics often are inconsistent, and often even the Communists themselves knew them to be false. But the Communists are not seeking truth; they are seeking power. They are not even seeking, primarily, to fulfill the prophecies of Karl Marx. What the Communists are after is the total destruction of existing civilization, so that they can build upon the ruins their own totalist political structure. They are playing the great fierce game of power, in which the stakes are innumerable human lives, and in which the prizes are total domination of all aspects of human existence. Therefore the Communists do not concern themselves with whether their arguments and their methods are "reasonable" or "humane."

Two Types of Revolutionary

Now what sort of person is the revolutionary, who is eager to, in the words of Gerhart Niemeyer, "disrupt, destroy, and distort most people's habits, preferences, and institutions"? In general, there are two types of revolutionary:

(1) The naïve or sentimental revolutionary, who believes that something is hopelessly wrong with life as we know it and that their revolutionary agenda actually can provide the remedy for all the ills to which humanity is heir. Though such a person is a dangerous dreamer, he may be sincere. Wherever a revolutionary party comes actually to power, such sentimental revolutionaries quickly are eliminated by their more realistic colleagues, as "Uto-

pians"—eliminated quite as ruthlessly as the "bourgeois obstructionists." But in countries like the United States, where such a radical, revolutionary regime never has attained power, it still is possible for some old-fashioned sentimental revolutionaries to survive side by side with hardcore, realistic ones. In such free states, the sentimental revolutionaries have not yet had all their illusions dispelled by the behavior of a revolutionary clique established in power; and the free, "capitalistic" government protects such sentimental revolutionaries, as it protects everyone else, from the purges of the majority of their kind.

(2) The realistic, practical revolutionary, who may employ humanitarian phrases to win converts, but whose real aim is pure power. These "realistic" revolutionaries constitute the majority of members of any revolutionary party. They are not really concerned with improving the state of existing society, or with lessening the confusion and disorder which form the recruiting area for them. Having observed the actual functioning of previous revolutionary regimes, they know quite well that they will not be humane or equalitarian or even efficient. These practical revolutionaries have lost all their illusions, and yet they remain hard-core revolutionaries. Some have gone too far to draw back without great personal danger; others, still less scrupulous, are willing to sacrifice everything in our civilization—including their own honesty—for the gratified lust of absolute power in their own hands and the hands of their clique. Like O'Brien in Orwell's novel *1984,* they are compensated by the pleasure of "stamping forever on a human face."

The revolutionaries have a track record. So, how is it that in many countries revolutionary radicals still make converts, and almost everywhere in the world they contrive to maintain an effective party organization, openly or underground, despite repeated disclosures of the inconsistency between their professions and their performance? The answer seems to be that the revolutionary movement is greatly assisted by popular ignorance and popular envy.

POPULAR IGNORANCE

Karl Marx expected that communism would triumph first in the more advanced countries of Europe and North America, where industrialism was far advanced and where general literacy prevailed. In actuality, communism triumphed in the less industrialized and less literate states: countries bewildered by the rapid advance of modern technology and social institutions, to which changes they were unable to adjust in any orderly fashion. In the confusion that ensued, the Communists rose to power. The principal gains of the Communists were in regions still less assimilated to twentieth-century life, and where still higher rates of illiteracy prevailed. Thus the Communists dealt, for the greater part, with peoples substantially ignorant of Russian history and current affairs, and therefore given to accepting Soviet claims at face value. But even in their dealings with the principal Western powers, the Communists were able to count upon a considerable degree of historical and political ignorance

among the citizens of free nations. The docility of the citizens
of free nations left—and leave—many among them prey to anti-
Western revolutionary movements. Minds ignorant of principle
easily are vanquished by ideology.

POPULAR ENVY

And where the abuse of ignorance will not suffice, the revolutionary resorts to the vice of envy. Envy, one of the most powerful and subtle of human emotions, is easily roused and difficult to repress. A man is not always aware of his own envy.
Kierkegaard remarks somewhere that envy is unconscious and
suppressed admiration. "Why should anyone else be more rich
or famous or popular than I am?"—in all of us there stirs at least
a little of this impulse.

So whenever an objection is raised to a revolutionary atrocity, the hardened revolutionary replies that the victims were "enemies of the people." The victims had property, and rank, and
prestige, and power; and so they deserved their fate, for presum-
ing to be better than you or me. When hundreds of thousands of
Ukranian peasants were shipped away in boxcars to die in the
Soviet arctic, the Communists attempted to justify this atrocity
before the world as retribution upon agricultural profiteers. When
uncounted thousands of Chinese were shot by Communist firing-
squads after the Communist military victory in China, this was
defended as the "liquidation of the selfish landlord class." (Most
of the "landlords" put to death had held less than ten acres of

land.)[1]

Yet these feeble and hypocritical excuses were accepted at face value by certain serious journals of opinion in America and Britain. It is easy, for a good many people, to conjure up a mental image of some Rich Bad Man who has to be shot because he stands in the way of the People's Progress. It is so hard for some people to confess to themselves that possibly the revolutionary ideologues are not kindly liberals who occasionally become a trifle impetuous. Envy, inverted admiration, is one of the most disastrous impulses of our modern age.

CANONS OF REVOLUTIONARY MOVEMENTS

The abuse of ignorance and the rousing of envy are the hardened revolutionary's usual tools. But he also has a set of formal doctrines with which to impress the educated and the half-educated. The revolutionary deliberately cultivates obscurity in language in order to make his arguments sound "scientific" and profound. Yet the principal dogmas of most revolutionary movements, especially Marxist inspired ones, can be set down quite simply and briefly. They are these:

(1) There is no God, and this life is the be-all and end-all. Therefore the material satisfaction of the masses is the only goal of life.

(2) All men and women ought to be equal in every way, especially in economic condition. "In order to establish equality," Marx, for example, wrote in *Das Kapital,* "we must first establish in-

equality." He meant that the Communist dictatorship would take away from the strong, the intelligent, the industrious, the thrifty, and the inheritors of property, and give to those less favored by nature. "From each according to his ability, to each according to his need."

(3) This revolutionary society is one of perfect equality. To establish revolutionary goals, any means is justifiable. The destruction of existing societies will be finally accomplished—after a period of subversion and gradual weakening—by violence. Then the "proletariat," the working classes, will establish a class dictatorship.[2]

(4) In time, this proletarian dictatorship will cease to be; the political state will wither away; and all mankind will live forever after in a classless, equalitarian, substantially changeless society, perfectly at peace.

(5) The only moral values are those of the proletariat, and the sole object of arts, literature, philosophy, and political activity is to wage the struggle of the proletariat against the "bourgeoisie," the middle classes. The revolutionary movement is an end in itself. It supersedes all religion, moral standards, and philosophy.

MEASURES TO ACCOMPLISH REVOLUTION

To accomplish revolutionary objectives, Marx and Engels listed in the *Communist Manifesto* (1848) the program of action that must be undertaken. All private property in land was to be confiscated; a heavy progressive income tax was to be put into effect; the right of inheritance was to be abolished; the property of all opponents was to be confiscated; the state was to monopolize banking and credit; the state was to monopolize communication and transportation; the state was to acquire factories and other means of production, and to improve the soil through collective farming; "industrial armies" were to be formed, with conscription of everyone for manual labor; agriculture and manufacturing were to merge; the state was to monopolize education and unite schooling with industrial production.

REVOLUTIONARY VIOLENCE

Wherever Marxist revolutionaries have come to power, they have put into effect these measures for the abolition of established society. But their primary means for destroying the church, the family, the community, lawful governments, private associations, and private property has been violence. Revolutionaries rarely have come to power peacefully, and they rarely tolerate political opposition or permit free elections. Their favorite method for attaining power is through subversion: working their way into the government of a country gradually, through intimidation and deceit, under the pretext of being merely one of several parties in a democratic state; and then, when sufficiently entrenched, resorting to the murder or imprisonment of all their opponents. In any country, including Russia and China, the members of the revolutionary party have formed only a very small percentage of the total adult population. The Communists, for example, deliberately keep their party organization small, for the sake of discipline and efficiency, and because they desire to rule the masses ruthlessly through the dictatorship of a clique. Again and again, the Communists demand the right to carry on their activities in free nations without restraint on the excuse that their party membership is so small as to offer no threat to established institutions. But the compact nature of Communist parties makes them the more dangerous. When the Communists seized power in Russia and China, they represented only a tiny fraction of the total population of those nations; yet they triumphed in very short order, once they had obtained control of the reins of government. The "liquidation"— that is, the murder or imprisonment—of all their opponents or of anyone who might remotely challenge their power, from monarchists to socialists, from cardinals to shopkeepers, was their first act once they obtained control over troops and police.

Revolutionaries Inspired by Hatred

The directing passion of most revolutionaries, in short, is hate. Christian compassion and Christian charity and Christian love are abhorrent to the revolutionary ideologue; so are the moral principles of Judaism and Islam and Buddhism and all other established religions. Appealing to the diabolical impulses in human nature, the revolutionary movements array class against class, man against man. Once triumphant, they perpetuate their clique in power by a system of police-spies and frequent purges of "deviationists" from their own ranks. Fear and suspicion torment everyone, from the most obscure working-people to the party leaders themselves. In the immediate background always looms up the vast concentration camp, to which are transported whoever may be accused of disloyalty toward the revolutionary regime, or even of lukewarmness toward its policies. Never before in the whole history of mankind has so large a proportion of any country's population been kept imprisoned as in the twentieth-century Communist states. Quite literally, Communist society is a living hell.

RADICAL ATTACKS ON AMERICA

Many revolutionary radicals seek to divert attention from their dismal caricature of Utopia by incessantly attacking, through elaborate propaganda, the alleged failings of free countries. The United States being the present chief check upon the radical ideologues' ambition, the accusations of their propaganda are directed with special intensity against America. Some of these charges may be summarized here.

(1) America is "materialistic": civilization in the United States is oppressed by a crass concentration upon private profit.

(2) America is "imperialistic": the United States intends to dominate all the other nations of the world.

(3) America is "capitalistic": American businessmen grow rich

upon the labor of the American poor.

(4) America is unjust: minorities and even majorities are repressed and bullied in the United States.

(5) America is decadent: public and private morality and culture are sinking toward utter collapse in the United States.

And there are other charges; but these five may suffice to illustrate the revolutionary methods in propaganda. Although nearly all Americans feel that these accusations are unfounded, too often Americans have failed to reply coherently to such charges. The revolutionaries' intention is to give Americans a bad conscience, and to give the United States a bad reputation in the rest of the world; to confuse, to obscure the revolutionary aim by a barrage of petty and reckless insults to the United States. The radical propagandists are satisfied if, though failing to convince altogether, they succeed in establishing doubts about American society in men's minds; for the objective is not so much to win adherents as simply to weaken loyalty to the United States and to dishearten America's allies.

[1] In a speech to Chinese Communist leaders in February, 1957, the Communist dictator of China, Mao Tse-Tung, admitted that eight hundred thousand people had been put to death by his regime during the four years after the nominal end of the Chinese civil war—that is, between 1949 and 1954. Other estimates of the numbers slain by Communist policy run far into the millions. Mao said, "In dealing with enemies, it is necessary to use force. We in China also have used force to deal with enemies of the people. The total number of those who were liquidated by our security forces numbers 800,000."

[2] Communist propagandists use the terms "communism" and "socialism" almost interchangeably. When indoctrinating Western prisoners, they usually employed the word "socialism" to describe the Soviet system, this having a sound less disagreeable to American ears.

Chapter Ten

THE AMERICAN ANSWER

America is unaccustomed to world leadership. We entered both World Wars only with great reluctance, and as a nation we have not sought to profit from our victories in those conflicts. Being new to many international responsibilities, sometimes we are hesitant and overly apologetic in our policies and statements; and sometimes we blunder. Nor is our society perfect, for no society ever has been perfect, or will be. Yet ours is a just, orderly, free, prosperous, and intelligent society. By the side of totalitarian societies, ours is a marvelous achievement. We have no need to damn ourselves with faint praise, though we ought not to fall into the opposite pit of braggadocio. Here, then, are some answers to the radical revolutionaries' accusations against the United States.

AMERICA AND MATERIALISM

(1) America is "materialistic" only in the sense that all men, everywhere, always have employed most of their time in getting and spending. American industry and thrift have helped to make

the United States the richest of great powers. And our material achievement renders possible a very high degree of leisure and cultural achievement among us. Honest private profit is a good thing: it produces "the wealth of nations," public prosperity.

There are many evidences that Americans are interested in much else besides getting and spending. We spend more upon formal education, per head of population, than does any other country. We have more churchgoers, per capita, than has any other great state. We have an immense number of public libraries and museums of art. We have one of the highest rates of literacy in the world. The intelligence and honesty of our popular newspapers is superior to that in most countries. In our brief span of national existence, we have acquired a national literature of a distinct character and universal meaning: the work of Nathaniel Hawthorne, James Fenimore Cooper, Herman Melville, Oliver Wendell Holmes, Mark Twain, Henry Adams, Henry James, Paul Elmer More, George Santayana, and many others. We have great private endowments for the advancement of culture.

AMERICA AND IMPERIALISM

(2) America is the least imperialistic, probably, of all great powers in all history. There is no American desire to build an empire overseas or in the Western hemisphere; nor do we attempt to secure trade monopolies abroad. We maintain garrisons in Europe and Asia to guard against the threat of foreign conquest of our allies, but we keep those forces at a minimum,

and withdraw them altogether whenever practicable. Sometimes, indeed, we may have acted with imprudence in giving up bases and positions important to our own security and that of our allies. We withdrew altogether from China after our war with Japan, for instance, even though the Communists were then engaged in overthrowing the Kuomintang government of China with which we were allied. We withdrew our troops from Korea despite Communist preparations for invading South Korea, and returned only after our small remaining forces had been attacked by the Communists. At the end of the war in Europe, we withdrew from eastern Germany, Czechoslovakia, and other territories, allowing the Communists to occupy those areas. These are not the actions of a nation bent upon building an empire.

Our whole national history refutes the charge that Americans mean to be masters of the world. When, in 1846, we utterly defeated the Mexicans, we did not annex Mexico, though we had taken their capital. In our war with Spain, in 1898, we did not annex Cuba, where most of the war was fought. Though we acquired the Philippines, we gave those islands complete independence after we had freed them from the Japanese at the end of the Second World War. Earlier in the twentieth century, we withdrew from Central America the Marines we had sent there to restore order. We took no part in the nineteenth- and twentieth-century partition of Africa, though we certainly had the power to do so. We maintain troops in Germany and Japan only at the request of those states. This is not the way in which an imperialistic country behaves.

Nor have we been economic imperialists. Opposed to monopolies and cartels, we have stood for commercial and industrial competition throughout the world, declining to take advantage of our military strength to secure commercial agreements favorable to the United States. To many nations, we give or lend far more than we sell to them or buy from them. Since the end of the Second World War, we have given many billions of dollars to other countries without expectation of repayment. Surely no imperialistic state ever followed this policy.

AMERICA AND CAPITALISM

(3) America is "capitalistic," and proudly so, in the sense that Americans believe in private property and private enterprise, and point to the fruits of that economic system. In earlier chapters of this book, we touched upon the merits of our free economy. It can stand upon its own record. It may also be emphasized that the American economy has been called a "people's capitalism," for ownership of property, including great industries, is very widely shared, and the profits go to the laborer as well as the owner and the manager. Private property is one of the chief satisfactions of life, Americans know, and private economic responsibility helps to secure public freedom.

AMERICA AND JUSTICE

(4) America is unjust only to the extent that perfect justice never has been secured anywhere, at any time in history. Justice is the securing to every man of what is his own. The civil rights and the property rights of Americans are guaranteed by federal and state constitutions, by the courts, and by centuries of usage. It is improbable that a greater measure of justice ever prevailed in any nation. There are regular means of redress for injustice: a man may appeal to the law, and to public opinion. Cases of injustice receive wide attention in America precisely because they are rare exceptions, not the rule. We take particular pains to preserve the rights of minorities; our constitutions, indeed, are intended primarily as a defense of minorities against hasty or selfish temporary majorities.

AMERICA AND DECADENCE

(5) Decadence, according to C. E. M. Joad, is "the loss of an object." A man is decadent who has ceased to have any aim in life; a society is decadent that no longer perceives goals and standards. Measured by this test, the United States remains a vigorous and hopeful society. Most Americans recognize objects in life. To do their duty under God; to rear decent families; to improve their own condition, and that of their community; to educate themselves; to acquire a home and other property; to maintain the best in their civilization—these goals con-

tinue to attract many millions of Americans. Foreign observers
are impressed generally with the vigor and strength of fiber in
American character. One of these, a Scot, Mr. J. M. Reid, once
remarked in the quarterly *Modern Age* that "freedom, simplic-
ity, and diversity" are the marks of American civilization. And
he continued:

> Thinking Americans are worried about many of
> the things that disturb us too—about the future
> of a civilization which seems, increasingly, to base
> its life and hopes on inessential gadgets, about
> the complications of industrialization, and tech-
> nology, and the hideous threat to life itself that
> these things have developed, about the weaken-
> ing, or absence, of traditional leadership and gen-
> erally accepted standards of culture. The very
> form that these worries take, however, is striking
> and even hopeful to a European. You still feel,
> as we once did, that the individual should be able
> to do something effective about the things that
> trouble him, whereas most of us have come to
> think that what is wrong with our world is be-
> yond our control—that our best hope is to es-
> cape disaster for ourselves, not to prevent it for
> the people and places we know. We feel our-
> selves to be already half-defeated, whereas your
> world still seems a manageable one, though it
> may be difficult to handle.[1]

No, America is not wholly the nation of Kinsey Report subjects, inane television-viewers, and Hollywood addicts that so much anti-American propaganda describes. The inventiveness, the industry, and the confidence in the goodness of life which are the symptoms of private and social health remain vigorous among us. Americans are willing to point out their own society's shortcomings, which is another indication that decadence is not upon us. A decadent man and a decadent people ordinarily confess to no faults, because they have lost sight of the standards by which virtue and vice are determined.

AMERICAN PROMISE

To save the rest of the world from this decadence, this revolutionary and collectivistic life-in-death, is a part of the American cause. "Observe good faith and justice toward all nations," President Washington wrote in his Farewell Address, more than two hundred years ago, to his fellow Americans. "Cultivate peace and harmony with all. Religion and morality enjoin this conduct; and can it be that good policy does not equally enjoin it? It will be worthy of a free, enlightened, and at no distant period, a great nation, to give to mankind the magnanimous and too novel example of a people always guided by an exalted justice and benevolence."[2]

America is a great nation; and if she is not invariably guided by an exalted justice and benevolence, still surely she is playing her part among the nations with some courage and generosity.

For two important reasons—and those of equal weight in the minds of most citizens of the United States—America has set her face against every totalist ideology, stationed her troops on foreign soil, built an immense air force and an immense fleet, poured out her national wealth in aid of the defense and the welfare of the free world. One reason is that Americans believe in the dignity of man, made in an image more than human; and the revolutionary ideologue threatens to destroy that dignity wherever he finds weakness. The other reason is that Americans know they themselves cannot be secure unless the civilization of which they are a part is secure. They do not hesitate to oppose by strength the armed doctrines of ideologues. Their cause, they believe, is the cause of true human nature, of enlightened order, regular justice, and liberty under law. For this cause they have made some sacrifices; they will make more.

Americans do not aspire to make the world into one vast uniform United States, for they cherish diversity at home and abroad. That our elaborate civilization and our delicate civil social order may not fall victims to the revolutionary movements at home and abroad: this is the end to which American policy is directed. And if Americans have valor in them still, theirs will not be a losing cause.

[1] J. M. Reid, "Three Words on America," *Modern Age*, Vol. 1, No. 1 (Summer, 1957): 80.

[2] Editor's note: See George Washington, "Farewell Address," in *American Presidents: Farewell Messages to the Nation*, ed. Gleaves Whitney (Lanham, Md.: Lexington, 2002).

THE AMERICAN ACHIEVEMENT
Gleaves Whitney

It has been almost a half century since Russell Kirk wrote *The American Cause.* At the beginning of the twenty-first century, what are we to make of the idea of "American exceptionalism," a concept that has served to guide much of the American experiment in ordered liberty since the Founding, and about which Kirk often reflected?

The idea of "American exceptionalism" was famously developed by Alexis de Tocqueville in *Democracy in America,* the most important book ever written about America by a foreigner. Tocqueville was a French aristocrat who came to our shores in the early 1830s. His pretext for coming here was to study prison reform. But he was really on the adventure of his life, and his observations of our communities and wilderness continue to yield rich insights 170 years later.

Tocqueville was highly educated; he knew that America was largely the product of Western civilization. But his travels convinced him that the U.S. was an exceptional nation, qualitatively different from European countries and considerably different from his native France. "In what part of human history can be found anything similar to what is passing before our eyes in North America?" he asked.

This is hardly to suggest that Tocqueville was uncritical. There were many things about our nation that he found problematic. But the upshot was this: whereas Europe represented the past, America represented the future. As countries around the world struggled toward more individual liberty, social equality, and constitutional democracy, they would increasingly look to, and look like, America.

Historians who read Tocqueville and ponder the American exceptionalism thesis sometimes find themselves drawing up their own list of ways in which America is different from other countries and civilizations. The re-publication of *The American Cause* provides an occasion for us to do the same. My aim is to set out what I believe are America's greatest historical achievements. My list is not taken to be exhaustive, universally shared, or unique to America. Yet it seems to me that each of these achievements is worth pondering because *each goes a long way toward overcoming some significant problem in the human condition.* For that reason I believe these achievements will pass the test of time. They are achievements that future civilizations might regard as enduring monuments to American greatness—enduring in the same way as are the moral greatness of the ancient Hebrews, the intellectual greatness of the ancient Greeks, the civic greatness of the ancient Romans, and the constitutional greatness of the medieval and early modern British.

(1) One great achievement of America is constitutional: America's Founders largely solved the age-old problem of constitutional instability. They knew the work of the ancient writer Polybius, who had described the problem of constitutional cycles in the ancient world. Polybius observed that most states mark their origins with the establishment of a monarchy. Things go well for a generation or two, but after a while the monarchy grows increasingly venal and degenerates into a tyranny. Then virtuous aristocrats revolt against the tyrant and establish themselves as the governing class. Things go well for a spell, but then the aristocracy grows self-indulgent and degenerates into an oligarchy. This causes the virtuous people to revolt against decadent oligarchs and establish a democracy. Then the people in their turn grow indolent and fickle and self-serving, degenerating into a mobocracy. It is apparent that there is a desperate need for order, and usually it comes by way of a charismatic leader bearing promises. He is crowned a king. Hence the restoration of the monarchy, only to start the cycle all over again. In this way the wheel of revolution goes round and round.

Many of America's founders believed there was an object lesson in this insight. When delegates to the Constitutional Convention met during that hot summer of 1787, they well knew their challenge. The burden was on them to create a constitution that was not susceptible to the cycle of revolution that was the affliction of past republics.

As Hamilton later wrote in *Federalist* 1, their challenge was also without historical parallel: "it seems to have been reserved to the people of this country, by their conduct and example, to decide the important question, whether societies of men are really capable or not of establishing good government from reflection and choice, or whether they are forever destined to depend for their political constitutions on accident and force."

Hamilton wrote that Americans of his generation would participate in one of the most fateful decisions any generation of humans anywhere had made. If the people chose wrongly, it would redound to "the general misfortune of mankind."

We know the outcome: the Constitution was ratified to the general good fortune of humankind. Our national charter was crafted such that the elements of ancient constitutions could check and balance each other: a kind of limited monarchy established in the Presidency; a kind of aristocracy established to a greater degree in the judiciary, to a lesser degree in the Senate; and a kind of democracy established in the House of Representatives.

In addition to these checks and balances at the national level, a federal structure was put in place to combine the best of a large entity like the Roman republic with the best of a small entity like the Athenian city-state. Enumerated powers defined the national government's sphere of responsibilities: defense, international treaties, immigration policy, and the like. States and communities retained their spheres of responsibilities: schools, welfare, public safety and health, and so forth.

The formula worked. The framers structured government in a way that ordered freedom to an unprecedented degree in world history. The divisiveness of human nature, which had been the undoing of many a republic, was accommodated in a brilliant fashion. We even came through a civil war with our Constitution largely intact. The ancient Greeks couldn't do that. The ancient Romans couldn't do that. Many modern nations cannot claim that achievement, either. The fact that Americans did is exceptional and ratifies the Founders' wisdom.

(2) Closely related to our Constitution is another great American achievement—recognizing human rights in word and deed. We take human rights for granted because we are Americans. I would venture that few, if any, readers of this book have been subjected to police raids or illegal detention in jail. I doubt that fewer still have been arrested for their religious beliefs or political opinions. We have rights that are recognized by our magistrates.

But throughout most of history, the majority of people have had few if any recognized rights. They have been slaves or serfs or subjects. It was kings who had rights—divine rights at that. America turned this idea on its head. In the United States, not kings but sovereign citizens would have divine rights, and these rights would be inviolable.

Human rights were advanced by numerous American documents, but I'd like to mention just three of them. The first was the Virginia Declaration of Rights, written largely by George Mason. It was adopted in June 1776 by a constitutional convention in the colony of Virginia. It declared that "all men are by nature equally free and independent and have certain inherent rights." No one could deprive fellow citizens or future generations of these rights, which included "the enjoyment of life and liberty, with the means of acquiring and possessing property, and pursuing and obtaining happiness and safety." Other specific liberties included freedom of the press, the free exercise of religion, and the injunction that no man could be deprived of liberty except by the law of the land or the judgment of his peers.

The second major document was produced less than a month later by another Virginian, Thomas Jefferson. It is widely recognized that the grand opening of the Declaration of Independence has been of incalculable influence in the modern age. Less widely known is that the specific complaints enumerated in the last two-thirds of the Declaration assume the ancient rights of Englishmen. The abstract universal rights at the beginning combined with the historically instantiated rights at the end make our Declaration powerfully comprehensive.

Both the Virginia Declaration and the Declaration of Independence were masterpieces that influenced political leaders on both sides of the Atlantic. They informed the third great document, our Bill of Rights, which comprises the first ten amendments to the Constitution. These were adopted *en masse* in December 1791. They are a collection of mutually reinforcing guarantees of individual rights and limitations on government.

It is important to see our Bill of Rights in historical context. Despite being associated with the American *Revolution*, it is a *conservative* document. It proposes no new rights, but ratifies already existing ones—to wit, the rights American colonists expected to enjoy as British subjects, but had not enjoyed because of London's arrogance. Some of these rights, like the right to bear arms, were medieval in origin. Others, like freedom of the press, had developed under a policy of salutary neglect. Whatever their origin, these rights were considered real in the minds of the Patriots—they could not be violated. From this perspective, we can see who the real revolutionary was in the American War of Independence. It was not George Washington. It was King George. He was the true revolutionary since it was his policies that violated the British constitution.

Many bills of rights have been generated since 1791. All are lovely proclamations. But ours is extraordinary. For ours went beyond the British Bill of Rights (1689) and was more historically grounded than the succeeding bills of rights it inspired (like the French Declaration of the Rights of Man and of the Citizen). As such, ours went a long way toward overcoming a significant problem in the human condition: the problem of government violating human dignity and rights with impunity.

(3) We got the Constitution right. We got the Bill of Rights right. But highfalutin words on paper are not enough. It has often been said that we cannot simply export our Constitution and Bill of Rights to other nations and expect them to take root. This is true. Two more things are needed, and America is exceptional to have both of them.

First, a people needs to understand what freedom is. We Americans are fortunate that the Founders and their generation possessed that understanding. They knew that freedom, per se, is not enough. They knew that freedom must be limited to be preserved. This paradox is difficult for many students to grasp. Young people generally think freedom means authority figures leaving them alone so they can "do their own thing." That's part of what it means to be free, but true freedom involves much, much more. As understood by our Founders and by the best minds of the young republic, true freedom is always conditioned by morality. John Adams wrote, "I would define liberty as a power to do as we would be done by." In other words, freedom is not the power to do what one can, but what one ought. Duty always accompanies liberty. Tocqueville similarly observed, "No free communities ever existed without morals." The best minds concur: there must be borders: freedom must be limited to be preserved.

What kinds of limits are we talking about?

• The *moral* limits of right and wrong, which we did not invent but owe largely to our Judeo-Christian heritage.

- *Intellectual* limits imposed by sound reasoning. Again, we did not invent these but are in debt largely to Greco-Roman civilization, from the pre-Socratic philosophers forward.

- *Political* limits such as the rule of law, inalienable rights, and representative institutions, which we inherited primarily from the British.

- *Legal* limits of the natural and common law, which we also owe to our Western heritage.

- Certain *social* limits, which are extremely important to the survival of freedom. These are the habits of our hearts—good manners, kindness, decency, and willingness to put others first, among other things—which are learned in our homes and places of worship, at school and in team sports, and in other social settings.

All these limits complement each other and make a good society possible. But they cannot be taken for granted. It takes intellectual and moral leadership to make the case that such limits are important. Our Founders did that. To an exceptional degree, their words tutored succeeding generations in the ways of liberty. It is to America's everlasting credit that our Founders got freedom right.

(4) Yet another thing needed to ensure the success of liberty is a vibrant civil society. Civil society has come to be defined as the whole network of non-governmental institutions that are created by people when they voluntarily associate with each other. It's the PTA, spelling bees, Rotarians, Knights of

Columbus, soup kitchens, Habitat for Humanity—the thousands of ways Americans freely come together.

Civil society is an idea with a fascinating history, traceable to Aristotle's *koinonia politike* and Cicero's *societas civilis*. By the time of Tocqueville, the notion was juxtaposed to two other realms of human association. First, there is the state, with its formal governing apparatus, from the White House to the state house to the courthouse. Then there is political society, which is comprised of mostly voluntary associations such as political parties, political action committees, lobbyists, and unions. Finally there is civil society *per se*, which essentially comprises the whole network of private and economic interests.

Tocqueville observed that civil society was much stronger in America than in Europe, and that it performed extremely valuable functions. Voluntary associations were filled with "super-abundant force and energy" to get things done. They were "the independent eye of society," enabling people to help one another without waiting for state action. In fact, they were an invaluable counterforce to the state.

What was true in Tocqueville's day continues to be true in our own. Despite signs of diminution, America continues to have the most vibrant, generous, far-reaching civil society in the world. It is the envy of other nations.

(5) Discussion of America's civil society naturally leads one to another, closely related achievement—and that is economic. We are only 6 percent of the world's population, yet we pro-

duce approximately 25 percent of the world's human-made things. Our economy is a colossus beyond the imagination's grasp, a dynamo that words cannot capture. Consider this: huge as it was just twenty years ago, our economy has more than doubled in size since then. No nation has ever had this experience. No nation has overcome the age-old problem of material privation or spread prosperity among the masses to the extent ours has.

Three elements would help launch our nation on the road to economic achievement. First, America's early development was unique among the nations in that it coincided almost exactly with the early stages of the Industrial Revolution. The Thirteen Colonies participated in this revolution since that revolution's origins were rooted in Britain.

Second, for many Americans economic success was a source of spiritual comfort. As the sociologist Max Weber observed, Calvinist theology taught that God blessed a predestined Elect. One sign of their election was worldly attainment. Joshua 1:8 speaks of God's faithful as being "prosperous" and "successful." Good, upright people work hard and try to acquire all the trappings of success in this life as a way of confirming their salvation in the next.

In addition to the Industrial Revolution and Calvinist theology, a third factor would start our nation on the road to economic achievement. It came in the form of a book that appeared coincidentally—some would say providentially—in the same year as America's founding, 1776. *The Wealth of Nations*, written by the Scottish moral philosopher Adam Smith, urged rulers to abandon the old mercantile system with its centralized planning and heavy-handed regulations. True prosperity would result from a free-market economy that imposed relatively few regulations and a low tax burden.

This is boilerplate for Americans—we take it for granted nowadays—but in 1776 it was bold to suggest that enlightened self-interest was the fundamental component of a dynamic economy. If people had more freedom, they would work harder. That hard work would generate a surplus, which they would invest to generate an even greater surplus. The resulting availability of capital would nurture new enterprises, new jobs, and new wealth. In this way material benefits would spread through society.

It must be said—this takes us back to the exceptionalism thesis—that America's success with free markets cannot be duplicated everywhere. Crucial to our economic achievement is the larger context in which that achievement has taken place. Among other things, that context includes the limits Americans recognize—the moral, constitutional, civic, and social limits that are part of our culture. A free-market economy can be sustained only where men and women recognize the entire culture of freedom. If that culture is lacking, if freedom is not ordered, capitalism can look pretty ugly. Certainly this has been the experience of countries where morality does not broadly leaven self-interest. Eastern Europeans, for example, bemoan the predatory "cowboy capitalism" running rampant in some parts of their world. Historian Gordon Wood notes, by contrast, how fortunate Americans have been historically. Our economy developed amid periodic great awakenings that kept people in touch with higher duties than raw self-interest. This helps explain why American philanthropy is one of the wonders of the world, dwarfing anything seen abroad or in the past.

(6) Our economic achievement helps explain another American achievement: the success with which America has attracted and absorbed huge numbers of immigrants. For more than two centuries, we have been the world's number one destination for people in search of a better life. More than 60 million people have voluntarily come to our shores. No other nation in world history has even come close to that. America represents the greatest voluntary migration of people in human history.

Tocqueville, because he himself was a foreigner and projected what it would be like to immigrate to the United States, was deeply impressed by this facet of American exceptionalism. In a striking passage he wrote that "emigration is incessant; it begins in the middle of Europe, it crosses the Atlantic Ocean, and it advances over the solitudes of the New World. Millions of men are marching at once towards the same horizon; their language, their religion, their manners differ; their object is the same. Fortune has been promised to them somewhere in the West, and to the

West they go to find it.

"No event can be compared with this continuous removal of the human race, except perhaps those eruptions which caused the fall of the Roman Empire. Then, as well as now, crowds of men were impelled in the same direction, to meet and struggle on the same spot; but the designs of Providence were not the same. Then every new-comer brought with him destruction and death; now each one brings the elements of prosperity and life."

One unintended consequence of the constant influx of foreigners into America has been a fascinatingly rich, multiethnic society.

America is not Shangri-la—there will always be interethnic tensions—but neither are we the Balkans. America is the most successful multiethnic society the world has ever seen. There have been others—ancient Egypt, Rome, the Austro-Hungarian Empire—but nothing rivaling America's achievement.

(7) I cannot prove it, but is it coincidental that the nation built by immigrants, by foreigners, has revolutionized foreign relations? For the last hundred years, America has been a formidable world power. For the last decade, we have been the lone superpower in the world. There is now a considerable body of evidence that we do not behave the way lone superpowers have behaved in the past.

If you study the superpowers of the past—Egypt, Assyria, Babylon, Persia, Rome, Spain, France, Germany, the Soviet Union—you see a ruthless self-interest at work. The goal of most superpowers is single-mindedly and relentlessly to impose their will on their neighbors. To build up the empire. To aggrandize the homeland. To crush rivals. There was rarely talk of building up a peaceful world community on the basis of mutual cooperation and moral suasion.

When Rome defeated Carthage, it burned the city and salted the surrounding fields so that Carthage could never rise again. When America defeated Germany in the most horrific war in human history, it made Germany the beneficiary of the Marshall Plan. This is extraordinary. Can there be any doubt that our practice of foreign affairs is rather exceptional among the nations?

There are other achievements that one could ponder: our powerhouses of higher education, the reach of our public libraries, the strength and stability of our middle classes, the technological empowerment of the common man, the decentralization of high culture throughout the land, and the instilling of an optimistic, can-do spirit among our people. What ties each of these achievements together is the extent to which it overcomes some persistent problem in the human condition. That is why the American achievement, writ large, will be an inspiration to future generations and civilizations.

America is no utopia, certainly. Yet it is more than just another country. In the perspective of world history, it is *exceptional*. As we ponder our founding, it is well for us to see the historically significant accomplishment America is. A renewed appreciation of our blessings will help Americans meet the many challenges we face, now and in the future.

SUGGESTED READING

For more on the founding and historical development of the United States, see:

Bernard Bailyn, *The Intellectual Origins of the American Revolution* (Cambridge, MA: Belknap, 1992).

Daniel J. Boorstin, *The Americans: The Colonial Experience* (New York: Random House, 1964).

———, *The Americans: The National Experience* (New York: Random House, 1988).

———, *The Americans: The Democratic Experience* (New York: Random House, 1974).

M. E. Bradford, *Founding Fathers: Brief Lives of the Framers of the United States Constitution*, 2nd ed., (Lawrence: University Press of Kansas, 1994).

———, *A Better Guide Than Reason: Federalists and Anti-Federalists* (New Brunswick, NJ: Transaction Publishers, 1994).

Orestes Brownson, *The American Republic: Its Constitution, Tendencies, and Destiny* (Wilmington, Del.: ISI Books, 2002).

Gary L. Gregg, ed., *Vital Remnants: America's Founding and the Western Tradition* (Wilmington, Del.: ISI Books, 1999).

Gerald N. Grob and George Athan Billias, eds., *Interpretations of American History: Patterns and Perspectives*, 6th ed., (New York: Free Press, 1992).

Russell Kirk, *America's British Culture* (New Brunswick, NJ: Transaction, 1993).
———, *The Roots of American Order* (LaSalle, Ill.: Open Court, 1974).

Harry V. Jaffa, *Crisis of the House Divided: An Interpretation of the Issues in the Lincoln-Douglas Debates* (Chicago: University of Chicago Press, 1999).

Pauline Maier, *American Scripture: Making the Declaration of Independence* (New York: Vintage Books, 1998).

Forrest McDonald, *Novus Ordo Seclorum: The Intellectual Origins of the Constitution* (Lawrence: University Press of Kansas, 1986).

Carl J. Richard, *The Founders and the Classics: Greece, Rome, and the American Enlightenment* (Cambridge: Harvard University Press, 1995).

Matthew Spalding, ed., *The Founders' Almanac* (Washington, D.C.: The Heritage Foundation, 2002).

George Tindall, *America: A Narrative History*, 2nd ed. (New York: Norton, 1988).

Alexis de Tocqueville, *Democracy in America*, trans. Harvey Mansfield and Delba Winthrop (Chicago: University of Chicago Press, 2002).

Gordon Wood, *The American Revolution: A History* (New York: Modern Library, 2002).

For more on moral and religious principles in American life, see:

Peter Berger, *A Rumor of Angels: Modern Society and the Rediscovery of the Supernatural* (New York: Anchor Books, 1970).

Hugh Heclo and Wilfred M. McClay, eds., *Religion Returns to the Public Square: Faith and Policy in America* (Baltimore: Johns Hopkins University Press, 2002).

James H. Hutson, Sara Day, Jaroslav Pelikan, eds., *Religion and the Founding of the American Republic* (Washington, D.C.: Library of Congress, 1998).

John Courtney Murray, *We Hold These Truths: Catholic Reflections on the American Proposition* (New York: Sheed and Ward, 1985).

Michael Novak, *On Two Wings: Humble Faith and Common Sense at the American Founding* (San Francisco: Encounter Books, 2001).

A. James Reichley, *Religion in American Public Life* (Washington, D.C.: Brookings, 1985).

Ellis Sandoz, *A Government of Laws: Political Theory, Religion, and the American Founding* (Columbia: University of Missouri Press, 2001).

———, ed., *The Political Sermons of the American Founding Era, 1730-1805* (Indianapolis: Liberty Fund, 1999).

Barry Alan Shain, *The Myth of American Individualism: The Protestant Origins of American Political Thought* (Princeton, N.J.: Princeton University Press, 1996).

For more on American political principles, see:

John W. Danford, *Roots of Freedom: A Primer on Modern Liberty* (Wilmington, Del.: ISI Books, 2000).

M. Stanton Evans, *The Theme Is Freedom: Religion, Politics, and the American Tradition* (Washington, D.C.: Regnery, 1994).

Bruce F. Frohnen, ed., *The American Republic: Primary Sources* (Indianapolis: Liberty Fund, 2002).

Alexander Hamilton, James Madison, John Jay, *The Federalist*, "Gideon edition," ed. George W. Carey and James McClellan (Indianapolis: Liberty Fund, 2002).

Ralph Ketchum, ed., *The Anti-Federalist Papers and the Constitutional Convention Debates* (New York: Mentor Books, 1996).

Russell Kirk, *The Conservative Mind: From Burke to Eliot* (Washington, D.C.: Regnery, 1993).
———, *The Politics of Prudence* (Wilmington, Del.: ISI Books, 1993).
———, *Rights and Duties: Reflections on Our Conservative Constitution*, 2nd ed. (Dallas: Spence Publishing, 1997).

Joseph Story, *A Familiar Exposition of the Constitution of the United States* (Washington, D.C.: Gateway Editions, 2000).

For more on free-market economic principles, see:
Peter Berger, *The Capitalist Revolution: Fifty Propositions about Prosperity, Equality, and Liberty* (New York: Basic Books, 1986).

Milton (and Rose) Friedman, *Free to Choose: A Personal Statement* (The Harvest Press, 1990).

F. A. Hayek, *Individualism and Economic Order* (Chicago: University of Chicago Press, 1996).

Russell Kirk, *Economics: Work and Prosperity* (Pensacola, Fla.: Beka Book, 1989).

Ludwig von Mises, *Socialism: An Economic and Sociological Analysis* (Indianapolis: Liberty Fund, 1981).

Wilhelm Roepke, *A Humane Economy; The Social Framework of the Free Market* (Wilmington, Del.: ISI Books, 1998).

Adam Smith, *An Inquiry into the Nature and Causes of the Wealth of Nations*, ed. R. H. Campbell, A. S. Skinner, and W. B. Todd (Indianapolis: Liberty Fund, 1982).

Thomas Sowell, *Basic Economics: A Citizen's Guide to the Economy* (New York: Basic Books, 2000).

For further perspective on the United States today and the world, see:
Dinesh D'Souza, *What's So Great about America?* (Washington, D.C.: Regnery, 2002).

Robert George, *The Clash of Orthodoxies: Law, Religion, and Morality in Crisis* (Wilmington, Del.: ISI Books, 2001).

Samuel P. Huntington, *The Clash of Civilizations and the Remaking of World Order* (New York: Touchstone Books, 1998).

Peter A. Lawler, *Aliens in America: The Strange Truth about Our Souls* (Wilmington, Del.: ISI Books, 2002).

Bernard Lewis, *What Went Wrong: Western Impact and Middle Eastern Response* (Oxford: Oxford University Press, 2001).

Roger Scruton, *The West and the Rest: Globalization and the Terrorist Threat* (Wilmington, Del.: ISI Books, 2002).

Index